Dining With the Stars

Dining With the Stars

A TASTE OF THE BEST

FOUR-STAR RECIPES FROM YOUR FAVORITE CELEBRITIES!

COMPILED BY
PAUL KENT DORN

POCKET BOOKS
New York   London   Toronto   Sydney   Tokyo   Singapore

POCKET BOOKS, a division of Simon & Schuster Inc.
1230 Avenue of the Americas, New York, NY 10020

ISBN: 0-671-01749-7

First Pocket Books hardcover printing December 1998

10   9   8   7   6   5   4   3   2   1

Printed in the U.S.A.

QF / ✖

Contents

Author's Introduction   xi

Foreword by Melba Moore   xiii

Preface by Rita Moreno   xv

Introduction by AIDS Project Los Angeles   xvii

Appetizers, Soups, and Salads

Annie Potts	Pan-fried Crab Cakes	2
Florence Henderson	Lasagna Rolls	4
Estelle Getty	Crispy Oven-baked Chicken Fingers	6
Jay Leno	Uncle Louie's Chicken Wings Marinara	8
Barbara Hale	Salmon Appetizers	10
Robert Guillaume	Guillaume Crab Cakes	12
Marty Ingels	Marty's Nutty Cheese Roll	14
Kenneth Cole	Eggs and Toast for the Well-Shod Male	16
Halle Berry	Almond-Berry Brie Appetizer	18
Joan Collins	Pheasant and Leek Soup	20
Dick Clark	Mushroom Soup	22
Casey Kasem	Vegetable Soup	24
Celeste Holm	Curried Chicken Soup	26
Rosalynn Carter	Cream of Broccoli Soup with no Cream	28

Frances Fisher	Gazpacho Soup	30
Eddie Albert	Corn Soup	32
Christie Brinkley	Brinkley's Beautifying Vegetable and Bean Soup	34
Shirley MacLaine	Favorite Chicken Soup	36
Linda Gray	Black Bean and Rice Salad	38
Kellie Williams	Mérida Salad	40
Jean Le Clerc	Fresh Mushroom Salad	42
Lee Holzapfel	Lee's Cucumber Salad	44
Burgess Meredith	Meredith Malibu Nacho Salad	46
Cristina Ferrare	Arugula Salad with Black Olive and White Bean Crostini	48

Entrées

Elizabeth Taylor	Spicy Chicken	52
Barbara Eden	Chicken Curry Casserole	54
Bob Hope	Favorite Chicken Hash	56
Phyllis Diller	Phyllis Diller's Chicken Charisma	58
Nichelle Nichols	Scallop Stir-fry	60
Elizabeth Hurley	Shepherd's Pie	62
Robin Leach	Silver and Gold Chicken	64
Isadora Alman	Isadora's Sweet and Sour Chicken	68
Mariette Hartley	Spaghetti Boyriven	70
Dom DeLuise	Broccoli with Rigatoni	72
Mike Burger	Mike's Lucky Chicken	74
Carnie Wilson	Fettuccine with Chicken	76
CCH Pounder	Charmaine Lewis's Fish Escabeche with Fruity Salsa	78

Rita Moreno	Beef Picadillo	80
Jane Leeves	Shepherd's Pie with Beef	82
Chevy Chase	Vegetable Lasagna	84
James Earl Jones	Chilean Sea Bass	86
Corliss Tillman	Shrimp Gumbo	88
Barbara Bush	Barbecued Chicken	90
Debbie Reynolds	Eggplant Casserole	92
Jayne Meadows and Steve Allen	Shrimp Flambé Newburg	94
Charles Perez	Stuffed Rice	96
Michael Feinstein	Peppery Pasta	98
Janet Leigh	Lamb Shanks	100
Regis Philbin	Joy's Pasta à la Passion	102
Joanne Woodward	Sole Cabernet	104
Jane Russell	Pepper Steak à la Jane Russell	106
Michele Lee	Shrimp Pasta à la Zefferelli	108
Liz Smith	Chicken-fried Steak	110
Peter Reckell	Chicken Vegetable Stir-fry	112
Morgan Fairchild	Pacific Red Snapper	114
Mary Frann	Braised Venison with Fruit Compote	116
Vic Damone	Linguine and Clams	118
Alana Stewart	Fettuccine in Pepper Cream Sauce	120
Rita Rudner	Spaghetti with Gummy Bears	122
	Exploding Potato	122
Donna Karan	Garlic Thyme Grilled Chicken	124
Zsa Zsa Gabor	Dracula Goulash	126
Joe Diffie	Chicken Spectacular	128

James Brown	Crab Bake Imperial	130
Shirley Jones	Shirley's City Chicken	132
Mitch Gaylord	Spicy Tuna Pasta	134
José Eber	Beef Bourguignon	136
Tracy Lawrence	B-B-Q Meatballs	138
Patti LaBelle	Barbecued Shrimp	140
Travis Tritt	Hot and Spicy Chili	142
Melba Moore	Melba Moore's Zingin' Singin' Chicken	144
Connie Stevens	Bolognese Sauce	146
Sally Kirkland	Sally's Tiger Shrimp in Mustard Sauce	148
Kim Fields Freeman	Great French Fries	150
Jacklyn Zeman	Gazpacho Pasta	152
Gloria Gaynor	Chicken à la Gaynor	154
Sharon Gless	Reza's Tandoori Chicken	156
Joanna Kerns	Joanna's Pasta with Broccoli and Leeks	158
Jo Marie Payton	One-pot Poultry Passion	160
Majel Barrett Roddenberry	Kumquat Chicken	162
Stefanie Powers	Pierogie	165
Hugh Hefner	Pot Roast Dinner	168
Buddy Hackett	Sweet-and-Sour Baked Fish	171
Nina Blackwood	Salmon in Pastry with Herb Sauce	174
Clint Eastwood	Spaghetti Western	177
Mary Wilson	Supremely Healthy Turkey and Black-eyed Peas with Couscous	180

Side Dishes

Lee Grant	Steamed Cabbage	184
	Applesauce	184
Lynn Tanner	Rum Pot	186
Audrey Meadows	Lazy Six Japanese Eggplant	188
James Cromwell	Sautéed Kale with Garlic and Bread Crumbs	190
Lee Meriwether	Kyle and Lesley's Sweet Potato Mellow Crisp	192
Dean Jones	Southern Corn Bread	194
Betty Ford	Blu'Bana Bread	196
Kathie Lee and Frank Gifford	Apple-Bran Muffins	198
Angela Lansbury	Famous Power Loaf	200
Patty Loveless	Cranberry Nut Bread	202
Nancy Reagan	Monkey Bread	204
Ashley Judd	Perfect Biscuits	206
Star Jones	Sweet Potato Pie	208
Caryl and Marilyn	Artery Bread	210

Desserts

George Hamilton	Chocolate Chip Cookies	214
Lady Bird Johnson	Lace Cookies	216
Jackie Collins	Orange Chocolate Cheesecake	218
Garrett Glaser	Aunt Emma's New England Rice Pudding	220
Rolonda Watts	Rolonda's Shakin' Quakin' Apple Cakin'	222
Geraldo Rivera	Amaretto Caramel Custard	224
Maureen McGovern	Fresh Fruit Cobbler	226

Sally Jessy Raphaël	Sally's Oatmeal Cookies	228
Nely Galan	Custard Cake	230
Nolan Miller	Southern Plantation Bananas	232
Abigail Van Buren	Abby's Famous Pecan Pie	234
Isaac Mizrahi	Chocolate Mousse	236
Leeza Gibbons	Mocha Almond Biscotti	238
Adam Wylie	Strawberry Pop Cake	240
Linda Evans	Peach Heaven	242
Dolly Parton	Stack Pie	244
J. Cynthia Brooks	Hungarian Palascinta	246
Vince Gill	Peanut Butter Fudge	248
Tom Jones	Brandy Snaps	250
Jamie Farr	Whiskey Cake	252
Buzz Aldrin	Peanut Butter Moon Pie	254
Beverly Garland	Chocolate Ladyfingers Ice Box Cake	256
Tippi Hedren	Marnie's Favorite Red Velvet Cake	258
Matrix of Wine and Food		262
Index		265

Author's Introduction

All the world's a stage,
And all the men and women merely players:
They have their exits and their entrances;
And one man in his time plays many parts

—WILLIAM SHAKESPEARE

In the Old West, when a cholera epidemic broke out, people chipped in and did whatever they could to stop the spread of the disease and to help the dying. Or they moved on. The ones who chipped in were usually those who had a stake in the afflicted community or region. Those who moved on were usually drifters or loners whose main concern was to look out for themselves. A few stayed to help from a sense of compassion. Most people who helped did so out of common sense.

Our planet is now threatened with a subtle and insidious organism, the AIDS virus. As the disease spreads, there are fewer and fewer places to which we can move on. People are afraid of AIDS. They are so afraid that many are ignoring the problem by telling themselves that it's only in the gay community, that it's not their problem.

As public awareness became more acute, mainly through the efforts of a few compassionate people, others came to realize that we were all at risk. Health workers were getting AIDS from needle sticks; patients were getting it from blood transfusions; even babies were being born with AIDS. Some people realized that they could become infected and not even suspect it. Some became compassionate. Others ignored the problem—the modern-day equivalent of moving on.

People who read this note are of three types, those who are HIV positive, those who are not but have or have had an infected loved one, and those with neither condition. To the first two groups, *Dining With the Stars: A Taste of the Best* may offer some consolation in the knowledge that someone is doing something constructive in the battle against this killer. To the third group, many of whom may not realize that the AIDS virus could mutate at any time into something that could threaten our entire civilization, this book offers a chance to take out some life insurance against such a disaster.

Dining With the Stars: A Taste of the Best is a wonderful cookbook, full of elegant and delicious recipes that will bring pleasure and enjoyment to anyone who uses them. And 50 percent of the net proceeds of the book's sales, unlike funds acquired by conventional methods, will go directly to AIDS support, education, and research. The compassionate will need little encouragement to help. For others, who may appear uncaring or fearful, here is an opportunity to use some common sense.

I had the great fortune to experience the excitement and adventure of extensive foreign travel while young and impressionable. By my mid-twenties, I had traveled to and lived in thirty-two countries. The memories are vivid and as varied as the lands where I lived and where I visited—the people, the customs, the sights, the sounds, the aromas. And, of course, the food.

I love to entertain and any event is an excuse for me to celebrate, be it a formal gourmet dinner or a backyard picnic. Over the years, my guests have asked me for recipes and advice about food preparation and menu ideas. But I soon realized something very important: While people enjoy interesting foods, they do not have—nor do they wish to spend—a great deal of time in the kitchen. And, once there, many people simply don't know what to do.

I have called upon my friends to help create *Dining With the Stars: A Taste of the Best*. It is a wonderful collection of easy-to-prepare recipes that will suit a variety of tastes and occasions. This star-studded cookbook includes many favorite family recipes as well as recipes from the personal chefs of the stars. With the help of my friends at the Robert Mondavi Winery, I have also added wine suggestions for all the recipes and have included a reference guide for wines, to help answer questions. *Dining With the Stars: A Taste of the Best* will help a novice or an experienced cook create, prepare, and serve a grand meal, whether for a formal party or a relaxed luncheon or picnic.

I truly enjoyed developing this cookbook. My fondest hope is that the profits from its sales, which are being given to AIDS support, education, and research, will help improve the lives of this and future generations.

—PAUL KENT DORN

Foreword

$\mathcal{E}$ach day, with its inevitable rise and fall of the sun, shows us Mother Nature's awesome power and the gifts from the Master, be they great or small. As the seasons change, children grow and we often marvel at their development, both mental and physical, and we applaud the ingenuity of mankind with its new technological and social developments.

However, the passing of days and the setting of the sun must also remind us of the pain and challenges that many of us face, especially those whose lives are hectic and difficult because of situations that they have little or no control over. Then, of course, we become more grateful for the simple things—a gentle breeze, that great telephone call, and precious memories that give us pleasure and make us smile because of the warmth and joy they evoke.

I am constantly touched and moved by the efforts our society has made on both the grand and small scale in the fight against Acquired Immune Deficiency Syndrome. We as a society have seemingly begun to embrace the teachings of the great Master of compassion, humility, and true love for our fellow human beings.

This disease has proven to know no boundaries, be they social status, age, creed, or sex. It truly does not discriminate and reminds us that as a people we must all be concerned for the lives surrounding us. As you read this book please be moved by the love and the depth of caring that you, its author, and all of the contributors share with those who are less fortunate. But please also be proud of the courageous fight and incredible inspiration each person with AIDS and HIV must have to continue to live and breathe, and to look to each new day as a new blessing.

I ask that each of us, while enjoying this book, take time to think of the lives that we are touching, the funds that are being raised, and the children who will eventually be able to look upon AIDS and HIV as challenges of our world that we were all a part of eliminating. One day we will all be able to refer to AIDS as a scourge of the past that we helped find a cure for, thanks to the philanthropic nature in all of us.

I am touched by the many lives that AIDS and HIV have played a part in. I have lost friends, acquaintances, and loved ones and have seen an enemy that many thought was the worry of only a few rise to prominence and affect every human being's life directly.

Please take time to focus on what a monumental effort this offering is and the fact that the age-old adage "United we stand, divided we fall" is more of a truth in our fight than ever before. Hug your loved ones; show them you care; give time and effort back to those who may have a few more challenges. But most of all, please applaud yourself for the role that you are taking as a soldier in the most unbelievable war of mankind's history.

With Love,

MELBA MOORE

Preface

This lovely book of recipes appeals to me on three levels.

First, it is about the preparation of food, an area that has always been of great interest to me. I love to cook, and these pages represent an adventure in good dining.

Second, the recipes in this book have been donated by many people in the arts, sports, and public office whom I have always admired.

And last, some of the profits derived from the sale of this collection of interesting recipes will be set aside to help victims of AIDS. Any enterprise that supports AIDS research or offers help to its victims deserves our support.

—RITA MORENO

Introduction

BY AIDS PROJECT LOS ANGELES

While you are enjoying reading ***Dining With the Stars: A Taste of the Best,*** know that you are helping improve the quality of life for thousands of people living with AIDS. For a substantial portion of the proceeds of Paul Kent Dorn's book will benefit AIDS Project Los Angeles.

AIDS Project Los Angeles is a nonprofit, community-based organization that is a direct provider of HIV/AIDS services and information. APLA is committed to serving people living with AIDS and their families and friends and to reducing the incidence of HIV transmission.

Currently, we are providing services for more than six thousand people living with AIDS. It is because of the generous contributions of people like Paul that we can improve the quality of life of our clients and try to reduce the incidence of future transmission through educational outreach.

The staff, clients, and volunteers of AIDS Project Los Angeles thank Paul Kent Dorn and you, the reader, for giving us the opportunity to continue our work.

—JAMES LOYCE JR.
Executive Director
AIDS Project Los Angeles

Appetizers, Soups, and Salads

ANNIE POTTS

ART STREIBER

Annie Potts's most recognized character is Mary Jo of the TV series "Designing Women." An excellent supporting actress, she has appeared in more than a dozen movies, including the *Ghostbusters* movies, *Pretty in Pink*, and *Who's Harry Crumb?*

Pan-fried Crab Cakes

(Serves 6)

⅓ cup sour cream
1 egg, beaten lightly
1 teaspoon minced garlic
½ teaspoon salt
½ teaspoon pepper
1 teaspoon curry powder
½ teaspoon cayenne
1 pound crabmeat
1 cup dry bread crumbs
6 tablespoons olive oil
Salsa, for garnish

Combine the first 9 ingredients in a large bowl and mix well. Form into 12 patties about 2 inches in diameter. Heat the olive oil in a skillet and sauté on both sides until lightly browned. Serve with salsa.

 =Robert Mondavi Winery Napa Valley Fumé Blanc

FLORENCE HENDERSON

FHB PRODUCTIONS

I love Italian food. As a matter of fact, I love Italians! They cook with a magic pot. No matter how many unexpected guests show up for dinner, the magic pot expands to feed them. Now that's amore!

☆

Outspoken in all areas of life, Florence Henderson is probably best known as the all-American mom, Carol, of "The Brady Bunch."

Lasagna Rolls

(Serves 4 to 6)

1½ cups chopped onion
2 garlic cloves, minced
2 tablespoons olive oil
2 cups ricotta cheese
1 teaspoon dried basil
1 teaspoon dried oregano
½ teaspoon salt
3 cups grated zucchini
½ pound lasagna noodles, cooked
3 cups tomato sauce
½ cup grated parmesan cheese

Sauté the onion and garlic in olive oil until soft. Let cool. Mix the ricotta cheese, basil, oregano, salt, zucchini, and the onion mixture together. Spread ¼ cup of the cheese mixture evenly on each noodle. Roll up the noodle and place it, on end, in a greased baking dish. Continue until all noodles are used. Pour tomato sauce around each roll but not over the tops.

Cover and bake for 20 to 25 minutes at 375 degrees. Sprinkle with parmesan cheese and serve.

 = Robert Mondavi Winery Napa Valley Pinot Noir

ESTELLE GETTY

The feisty Sicilian of "The Golden Girls," Estelle Getty is one of the finest character actresses in the business.

Crispy Oven-baked Chicken Fingers

(Serves 8 to 10)

Olive oil cooking spray
3½ cups pecan meal
2 cups dry bread crumbs
1 tablespoon salt
1 tablespoon Cajun seasoning
2½ pounds boneless, skinless chicken breasts, cut into chicken fingers
2 large eggs, beaten

Spray 2 jelly-roll pans with olive oil. Combine the pecan meal, bread crumbs, salt, and Cajun seasoning in a large bowl and mix well. Dip chicken pieces in eggs and dredge in pecan mixture. Place on jelly-roll pan and spray with olive oil.

Bake at 450 degrees on both racks, switching pans between racks halfway through, for 35 to 40 minutes, or until the chicken is golden brown and juices run clear.

= *Robert Mondavi Winery Napa Valley Chardonnay*

JAY LENO

Jay Leno is an Emmy-winning talk show host and comedian. His fifth-grade report card is said to have read, "If Jay spent as much time studying as he does trying to be a comedian, he'd be a big star." Jay is also an avid car collector.

Jay Leno

Uncle Louie's Chicken Wings Marinara

(Serves 4 to 6)

2 to 3 pounds chicken wings
Flour, for dredging (optional)
Safflower or peanut oil, for deep-frying (optional)
Olive oil
Garlic cloves, crushed, or garlic powder, to taste
1 large can Italian plum tomatoes
1 tablespoon chopped parsley
Salt, to taste
2 tablespoons hot sauce, or more to taste

Cook the chicken wings by broiling or lightly flour them and deep-fry in hot oil. While they are cooking, prepare the sauce.

Heat a film of olive oil in a pan, add the crushed garlic or garlic powder. Mash the canned tomatoes through a sieve and cook in the olive oil. Add the parsley and salt, then cook for about 20 minutes. At the end of this cooking time, add the hot sauce (put in a little or a lot, depending on how hot or mild your taste, but put in at least 2 tablespoons, or the sauce won't be as tasty). Cook for 3 to 4 minutes more.

Toss the chicken wings in a bowl with ½ cup of the sauce and serve the remaining sauce on the side for dipping. Enjoy!

=Robert Mondavi Winery Napa Valley Pinot Noir

BARBARA HALE

One of the mainstays of the entertainment industry, Barbara Hale is best known for her role as Della Street, Perry Mason's right-hand woman. Her acting career includes some wonderful movies: *And Baby Makes Three*, *The Boy with Green Hair*, and *Far Horizons*.

Hi Paul —
Do try this — It's
yummy!
Good Luck.
Barbara Hale

Salmon Appetizers

(Makes about 40 appetizers)

1 can (15 ounces) salmon or 2 cups cooked salmon, flaked
1 package (8 ounces) cream cheese, softened
4 tablespoons mild or medium salsa
2 tablespoons chopped fresh parsley
1 teaspoon chopped fresh cilantro
¼ teaspoon ground cumin (optional)
8 flour tortillas (8 inches)

Drain the salmon, removing any bones. Combine the salmon, cream cheese, salsa, parsley, and cilantro in a small bowl. Add the cumin, if desired. Spread 2 tablespoons of the salmon mixture over each tortilla. Roll each tortilla up tightly and wrap individually with plastic wrap. Refrigerate for 2 to 3 hours.

Slice each tortilla into bite-size pieces.

First of all, I am proud to be part of this wonderful collection and its support of AIDS Project Los Angeles. Whenever I entertain, my appetizer is a never-fail recipe for any hors d'oeuvre tray. In fact, I used to take a tray of these to the set for the crew, and as a rule they would disappear. I would always find them in Raymond Burr's dressing room!

=Robert Mondavi Winery Napa Valley Chardonnay

ROBERT GUILLAUME

A legitimate theater actor, Robert Guillaume did Andrew Lloyd Webber's *The Phantom of the Opera*, but he is more recognizable to the younger generation for his roles in the TV series "Benson" and "Soap." Chevy Chase and Goldie Hawn fans will recognize Robert from the movie of Neil Simon's *Seems Like Old Times*.

Guillaume Crab Cakes

(Serves 8)

3 cups lump crabmeat
½ cup finely chopped carrots
½ cup finely chopped celery
½ cup finely chopped green bell pepper
½ cup finely chopped yellow bell pepper
½ cup finely chopped red bell pepper
½ teaspoon cayenne
2 tablespoons chopped parsley, fresh
½ teaspoon chopped basil, fresh
1 to 2 eggs, beaten, enough to make cakes stick
Salt and pepper, to taste

Bread crumbs, flour, or cracker meal, for dredging
2 to 3 tablespoons vegetable oil, for sautéing

Mix together all the ingredients for the crab cakes and form cakes about ½ inch thick and 4 inches in diameter. Roll in bread crumbs, flour, or cracker meal. Heat the oil in a skillet over low to medium heat and sauté the crab cakes until golden brown on both sides.

 = Robert Mondavi Winery Napa Valley Sauvignon Blanc

MARTY INGELS

Marty Ingels, a Brooklyn-born comedian, became a stage, film, TV, and nightclub entertainer after a two-year apprenticeship in show business. He has played comic parts in films since the early sixties. One of his best known movies is *If It's Tuesday, This Must Be Belgium*. Marty runs a successful talent agency booking stars for commercials. He is married to the actress Shirley Jones.

MARTY INGELS

Marty's Nutty Cheese Roll

(Makes 2 cups)

1 package (8 ounces) cream cheese
2 ounces blue cheese
4 ounces shredded sharp cheddar cheese
¼ teaspoon garlic powder
Dash of Worcestershire sauce
1 tablespoon brandy
1 tablespoon sherry wine
Dash of white pepper
1 cup chopped walnuts

Blend all the ingredients except the walnuts. Make into a ball and roll in the chopped nuts. Cover with plastic wrap and refrigerate for 2 hours.

=Robert Mondavi Winery Coastal Cabernet Sauvignon

KENNETH COLE

Footwear and accessory designer Kenneth Cole founded his company in 1982. Since then, he has become world famous as a fashion entrepreneur and has been honored as one of the most astute businesspeople in the fashion industry. His awards include the 1985 and 1987 Cutty Sark Men's Fashion Award, the 1994 GLAAD (Gay and Lesbian Alliance against Discrimination) New York Media Award for outstanding achievement in advertising, and the 1994 Extraordinary Voice Award. Kenneth was named the 1995 New York City Entrepreneur of the Year and has served on the board of AmFAR (American Foundation for Aids Research) and the homeless project H.E.L.P. (Housing Enterprise for the Less Privileged) for many years.

KENNETH COLE PRODUCTIONS

Eggs and Toast for the Well-Shod Male

(Serves 1)

2 blobs of butter
Band-Aids
Cold water
3 eggs
Paper towels
Salt and pepper, to taste
2 slices of bread

Stand at the stove in a badly lit kitchen wearing nothing but shoes, black dress socks, and boxer shorts. Melt 1 blob of butter in pan. Cook on high so it gets done faster. Splatter hot butter on forearms. Rinse forearms under cold water. Apply Band-Aids. Discard burnt butter. Lower flame. Add more butter. Crack two of the eggs into the skillet with one hand, using a deft, quick wrist motion. Toss shells into kitchen sink. Sing *"Volare."* Dance around. Drop other egg on the kitchen floor. Curse. Mop up with paper towels. Stare at eggs in skillet until small bubbles appear on top. Flip with spatula. Add salt and pepper. Meanwhile toast bread in toaster. When finished, if it's a color other than black, sit back, take off your shoes (not recommended for everyone), and enjoy the meal.

 = *Woodbridge Zinfandel*

HALLE BERRY

REVLON INST.

This Revlon beauty's face is familiar to everyone because of her work in commercials. Halle Berry's film credits include parts in *Father Hood, Executive Decision, Bulworth* with Warren Beatty, and *Why Do Fools Fall in Love?*

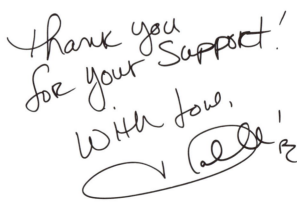

Thank you for your support!
With love,
Halle B

Almond-Berry Brie Appetizer

(Serves 10 to 12)

1 wheel (15 ounces) brie cheese
2 tablespoons raspberry jam
3 tablespoons brown sugar
1 tablespoon honey
¼ cup sliced unblanched almonds
Crackers or shortbread cookies, for serving

Slice the brie horizontally in half. Place the bottom half on a baking sheet. Combine the raspberry jam, 2 tablespoons of the brown sugar, and the honey in a bowl. Spread the mixture over the brie on a baking sheet. Top with the remaining brie half. Sprinkle with the almonds and the remaining 1 tablespoon brown sugar. Bake at 375 degrees for 10 minutes, or until soft. Then broil for 3 minutes, or until bubbly and browned. Serve with crackers or short-bread cookies.

 =Robert Mondavi Winery Coastal Johannisberg Riesling

JOAN COLLINS

Joan Collins is not just glamour and beauty; she is a true humanitarian. She is an honorary member of the National Society for Prevention of Cruelty to Children, a patron of the International Foundation for Children with Learning Disabilities, and sponsor of the Joan Collins Wing of the Children's Hospital of Michigan. Winner of the coveted Golden Globe and People's Choice awards, Joan has appeared in more than fifty feature films and twenty-five television programs. She is best known as the sassy vixen Alexis Carrington Colby from the world-famous evening drama series "Dynasty."

JOAN COLLINS

Pheasant and Leek Soup

(Serves 6)

1 pheasant (3 pounds), breast removed and carcass chopped into 6 sections
2 tablespoons olive oil
Salt and pepper, to taste
4 ounces finely chopped bacon
3 cups sliced leeks
1 cup chopped carrot
½ cup chopped celery
1 cup seeded and chopped tomato
1 bay leaf
¼ cup chopped basil
1 cup chopped portobello mushroom
1 cup red wine
5 cups chicken stock
1 tablespoon balsamic vinegar
½ cup chopped cilantro

Remove the skin from the pheasant breast, coat with olive oil, and season with salt and pepper. Set aside. Sauté the bacon in a heavy skillet until crisp, remove, and drain on paper towels, reserving the drippings. Add the leeks, carrot, celery, tomato, bay leaf, basil, mushroom, and pheasant carcass. Sauté for 3 to 5 minutes, then add wine and stock. Bring to a boil and simmer for 45 minutes, occasionally skimming fat that rises to the top. Remove the pheasant carcass, pull off any meat and return it to the pot, discarding the skin and bones. Broil or grill skinless pheasant breast until medium rare, 4 to 5 minutes on each side. Set aside. Add the vinegar to the soup. Thinly slice the breast. Ladle soup into bowls. Place meat on top and garnish with cilantro. Serve immediately.

=*Robert Mondavi Winery Napa Valley Pinot Noir Reserve*

DICK CLARK

My wife and I work together at the company and no matter how late we get home, we fix a gourmet dinner (with candlelight and wine). We usually prepare this soup the night before, since soups always seem to taste better the following day. This is our form of relaxation after our hectic days at the office.

☆

Often called America's oldest teenager, Dick Clark hosted "American Bandstand" and brought modern music into America's living rooms in the summer of 1957. He was inducted into the Rock and Roll Hall of Fame in 1993. Dick and his wife are hard workers, on the go most of the time. They love good food, well prepared.

Best wishes

Dick Clark

Mushroom Soup

(Serves 4)

1 onion
1 garlic clove, split
3 tablespoons butter
1 tablespoon olive oil
1 pound mushrooms
¼ cup tomato paste
5 cups chicken stock
1 teaspoon marjoram
Salt and pepper, to taste
1 teaspoon lemon juice
3 tablespoons red wine

Mince the onion in a food processor. Cook the onion and garlic in a heavy saucepan in I tablespoon of the butter and the olive oil until just beginning to brown. Discard the garlic. Separate the mushroom stems from the caps. Mince the stems and I cup of the caps in a food processor. Add the onions. Transfer to a bowl and set aside.

Fit the food processor with the slicing disk. Carefully place the remaining mushroom caps in the feed tube and gently push through to obtain even slices. Put the remaining 2 tablespoons butter in a sauté pan, add the onion mixture, and sauté for about 5 minutes. Add the tomato paste and stock, mixing well. Add the marjoram, salt, pepper, lemon juice, and wine and simmer for 10 minutes. Taste for final seasoning and serve.

 =Robert Mondavi Winery Coastal Pinot Noir

CASEY KASEM

CASEY KASEM

Become a vegetarian. Your body will respect you for your wisdom—and the animals will love you for your compassion.

☆

Casey Kasem set the standard for all countdown shows. He has the most successful format ever developed. With "American Top 40 with Casey Kasem" he reaches over 350 stations across America. Casey has the unique ability to accent each show with interesting stories about the artists and their rise on the charts along with listeners' dedications and long-distance requests from around the world. He also has an extensive TV and movie background.

Vegetable Soup

(Serves 12)

1 package (10 ounces) frozen green beans or 1 pound fresh green beans, cut into 1-inch lengths

1 green bell pepper, seeded and sliced or chopped

3 large carrots, chopped

4 large zucchini, chopped

½ large or 1 small cauliflower, cut into florets

6 stalks celery, sliced

2 to 4 large onions, sliced or chopped

1 can (16 ounces) peeled tomatoes

1 (46 ounces) can V8 juice

½ teaspoon thyme

1 package (10 ounces) frozen whole baby okra (optional)

Combine all the ingredients, including okra, if using, in a large soup pot and simmer for 15 minutes. (This makes a large pot of soup; it will keep for a week in the refrigerator, covered.)

 =Robert Mondavi Winery Napa Valley Pinot Noir

CELESTE HOLM

Every recipe has a theme on which every chef can improvise!

☆

Celeste Holm, star of motion pictures, the Broadway stage, and television, was nominated for an Academy Award several times and won an Oscar for *Gentleman's Agreement*. She has a reputation for compassion and integrity and has long been an advocate and supporter of mental health programs. She regularly contributes to the work of UNICEF. Ms. Holm is currently appearing in the TV series "Promised Land."

CELESTE HOLM

Curried Chicken Soup

(Serves 6 to 8)

2 tablespoons butter

2 tablespoons extra virgin olive oil

1 small onion, diced

2 large carrots, diced

3 large stalks celery, diced

½ green bell pepper, seeded and diced

1 cup chopped tomatoes, preferably plum tomatoes

1 large Granny Smith apple, diced

1½ to 2 cups 1-inch breast pieces chicken, uncooked

⅓ cup all-purpose flour

1 tablespoon curry powder, or to taste

½ teaspoon ground nutmeg

Pinch of ground cloves

6 to 7 cups chicken stock or broth

Salt and pepper, to taste

1 cup raw rice, preferably Texmati

⅓ to ½ cup dried currants, to taste

Melt the butter with the oil in a soup pot. Add the onion, carrots, celery, and green pepper and sauté for 5 minutes. Add the tomatoes, apple, and chicken and sauté for 10 minutes more. Mix the flour with the curry powder, nutmeg, and cloves. Add enough stock to make a watery paste. Add to pot and cook over low heat for 5 minutes, stirring occasionally. Add salt and pepper. Add the remaining stock, partially cover, and simmer for 30 to 40 minutes, stirring occasionally. Taste and correct the seasoning. Set aside.

Cook the rice. When done, add the currants to the top of the rice. Replace the cover and keep covered until ready to serve.

Add the rice and currants to the pot of soup and serve in warmed bowls. Or ladle soup over the rice in individual bowls, which is what I prefer to do.

=Robert Mondavi Winery Coastal Chardonnay

ROSALYNN CARTER

Rosalynn Carter was our First Lady from 1977 to 1981 and played a significant role as advisor to her husband. She was honorary head of the President's Commission on Mental Health. Mrs. Carter advocates for better care for the elderly and is well known for her work with Habitat for Humanity, where she can often be found working side by side with the poor building homes. Her best-selling autobiography is titled *First Lady from Plains.*

RICK DIAMOND

With best wishes,
Rosalynn Carter

Cream of Broccoli Soup
with no Cream

(Serves 4)

1 medium onion, chopped
1 garlic clove, crushed
1 tablespoon sunflower or other vegetable oil or vegetable oil cooking spray
1 bay leaf
1 pound broccoli, chopped
2½ cups vegetable stock or broth
1 small potato, peeled and cut into chunks
Salt and pepper, to taste
Juice of ½ lemon
Low-fat plain yogurt

Sauté the onion and garlic in the oil with the bay leaf until soft, or in a saucepan sprayed with vegetable oil, for 3 to 4 minutes. Add the broccoli, stock, and potato, and simmer gently, covered, for 10 minutes, or until the broccoli is tender but still bright green. Remove the bay leaf and let cool a little.

Purée in a blender until not totally smooth. Season with salt and pepper and add lemon juice to taste. Reheat in a clean pan before serving if necessary. Add a dollop of yogurt just before serving.

=Robert Mondavi Winery Napa Valley Fumé Blanc

FRANCES FISHER

Frances Fisher has appeared in more than twenty-three features, including *Titanic, Pink Cadillac,* and *Strange Luck.* She also has a love for the theater and has appeared in more than a dozen stage productions.

CYNTHIA MACADAMS

Gazpacho Soup

(Serves 2)

6 medium-size ripe tomatoes, peeled, seeded, and coarsely chopped
1 medium onion, quartered
1 medium cucumber, peeled, seeded, and quartered
2 garlic cloves, peeled
½ teaspoon salt
¼ teaspoon pepper
3 dashes of Tabasco sauce
1 tablespoon extra virgin olive oil

Place all the ingredients in a blender and pulse until almost smooth.

As a single working mom, I have found eating on the run sometimes becomes a way of life. This recipe is a low-fat, low-calorie way to fill my tummy with vitamins and ward off colds until I can slow down to try out the other fabulous recipes in this book!

=Robert Mondavi Winery Stag's Leap District Sauvignon Blanc

EDDIE ALBERT

Stay healthy by eating organically!

☆

Eddie Albert, a consummate actor, has appeared in more than sixty features and may be best remembered for his role in "Green Acres." He also served as a Navy lieutenant during World War II. Nominated twice for an Academy Award, in 1994 he was honored with a Distinguished Public Service Award. Eddie has received many other awards for his humanitarian work as well.

Corn Soup

(Serves 6)

1 cup finely chopped onion
1 green bell pepper, seeded and diced
1 red bell pepper, seeded and diced
2 poblano chilies, seeded and diced
Peanut oil, for sautéing
4 to 6 ears of white corn, kernels only
4 cups chicken stock
4 cups cream sauce, flavored with bourbon if desired
Salt and white pepper, to taste
Chopped fresh sage and cilantro, to taste

Sauté the onion, bell peppers, and chilies in oil. Add the corn and cover the pot so corn can steam. Add the stock and cream sauce and cook until the corn is tender, about 5 minutes. Season with salt and pepper, sprinkle with sage and cilantro, and serve.

 = *Woodbridge Chardonnay*

CHRISTIE BRINKLEY

CHRISTIE BRINKLEY

This is my favorite soup!
☆
Christie Brinkley is a model and actress. Christie's all-American good looks and business savvy have propelled her to success as one of the world's most recognizable models.

Cheers!
Christie Brinkley

Brinkley's Beautifying Vegetable and Bean Soup

IT'S A WHOLE MEAL!

(Serves 10 to 12)

2 sweet potatoes, chopped bite size
2 baking potatoes, chopped bite size
4 carrots, chopped bite size
½ cup beans—green, red, kidney, or black
1 yellow squash, sliced
1 green zucchini, sliced
1 yellow bell pepper and 1 red bell pepper, chopped

Pour enough olive oil into a large soup pot to cover the bottom of the pot. Sauté 2 to 3 cloves garlic sliced lengthwise (the more you use the tastier) until golden. Remove the garlic slices and set aside. Add 1 chopped onion to the garlicky oil. Once onions are translucent, throw the garlic back in and add 4 cans of vegetable broth (be careful to choose broth that does not contain palm oils.). Once this boils add the sweet potatoes, baking potatoes, and carrots. Finally add fast-cooking veggies, such as the yellow squash, the zucchini, and the yellow and red bell peppers. Add ½ cup cooked or canned green beans or red, kidney, or black beans at the last minute so they don't fall apart.

Serve the soup up nice and hot, topped with lots of fresh cilantro to garnish.

Tips: You may need to add more broth or water, depending on how you prefer your soup. Add salt and pepper to taste. You can freeze this soup.

= Robert Mondavi Winery Coastal Merlot

SHIRLEY MACLAINE

Four-time nominated, one-time winner of the Academy Award (for *Terms of Endearment*) Shirley MacLaine has appeared in more than forty films, including *Sweet Charity*, *The Turning Point*, *Irma la Douce*, and *The Apartment*.

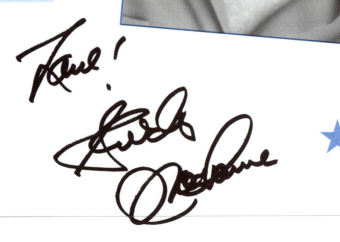

SHIRLEY MACLAINE

Love!

Shirley MacLaine

Favorite Chicken Soup

(Serves 4)

1 small chicken (2½ to 3 pounds), liver reserved
1 garlic clove, crushed
1 teaspoon ground coriander
1 teaspoon freshly ground black pepper
4 ounces mushrooms, trimmed and sliced
Oil, for frying
1 teaspoon soy sauce

Cook the chicken in water to cover until tender, 45 minutes to 1 hour. Remove from the broth. Remove the skin and bones and return the bones to the broth. Simmer for about 2 hours. Strain the broth. You should have about 4 cups; if not, add water. Cut the meat into small pieces and set aside.

Fry the garlic, coriander, and pepper in a little oil. Add the mushrooms, chicken meat, and the chicken liver. Add the broth and soy sauce and simmer for 10 to 15 minutes. Stir well and serve. Enjoy!

 = Robert Mondavi Winery Coastal Chardonnay

LINDA GRAY

Linda Gray got her first big role as Sue Ellen in the television series "Dallas" and has appeared on "Melrose Place."

LINDA GRAY

Black Bean and Rice Salad

(Serves 4)

2 cups raw basmati rice
2 tablespoons cumin, garlic powder, and Mexican seasoning
½ teaspoon salt
2 cups cooked black beans
4 plum tomatoes, seeded and diced
2 avocados, peeled and diced
1 small red onion, diced
1 bunch of cilantro, leaves chopped
2 bell peppers, yellow or red, seeded and chopped
1 tablespoon chili powder
Lemon or lime juice, to taste

Cook the rice as directed on the package, adding the cumin, garlic powder, Mexican seasoning, and salt to the cooking water. When the rice is done, cool and refrigerate until ready to serve.

Mix the rice, beans, and the rest of the ingredients except the lemon or lime juice in a large serving bowl. Add more seasoning as desired. Squeeze the lemon or lime juice on top.

 =*Robert Mondavi Winery Coastal Chardonnay*

KELLIE WILLIAMS

HARRY LANGDON

Kellie Williams plays the popular Laura Winslow on "Family Matters" and is in the feature film *Ride*.

Mérida Salad

(Serves 6)

1 cup cubed cooked chicken
3 large tomatoes, chopped
3 avocados, peeled and chopped
5 scallions, finely chopped
½ cup chopped canned ripe black olives
½ cup chopped canned green chilies
4 tablespoons olive oil
2 tablespoons apple cider vinegar
1 teaspoon salt
½ teaspoon garlic powder
¼ teaspoon pepper
1 medium head curly escarole, shredded
2 cups sour cream
2 cups shredded Monterey Jack cheese

Combine the first 6 ingredients in a large bowl, mix well, and set aside. In a small bowl, combine the olive oil, vinegar, salt, garlic powder, and pepper, mix well, and drizzle over the chicken mixture. Cover and refrigerate for 2 to 3 hours.

Arrange the escarole on serving plates. Spoon chicken mixture on top of escarole and top with sour cream and shredded cheese.

=Robert Mondavi Winery Napa Valley Pinot Noir

JEAN LE CLERC

Jean Le Clerc played popular artist Jeremy Hunter on the ABC-TV shows "Loving" and "All My Children." Jean is a member of the theater community, active as a producer and actor.

BRIAN APPEL

Fresh Mushroom Salad

(Serves 4)

8 ounces white mushrooms, stems removed
3 scallions, trimmed
Generous handful of parsley, finely chopped
Salt and pepper, to taste
½ lemon
2 tablespoons heavy cream

*F*inely slice the mushrooms and scallions and place in a serving bowl. Add the parsley and salt and pepper and squeeze the juice of ½ lemon over all. Toss. Add the cream and toss. Serve.

 =Robert Mondavi Winery Napa Valley Fumé Blanc

LEE HOLZAPFEL

Coming from an Orthodox Jewish home, I had never eaten bacon—however, once I was married I decided that I'd make bacon one morning for breakfast. So—I took out my frying pan, added some fat . . .

☆

Lee Holzapfel has worked on stage, television, radio, and film. Lee received her formal training in her hometown of London, England. As the wife of an American diplomat, she has traveled extensively and has entertained, not only audiences onstage, but also dignitaries in her home—often around her own dinner table. Lee prepared all the food for these functions herself—whether she was serving two guests or one hundred. She has recently appeared in *Murder at 1600, Contact, Mars Attacks,* and *Washington Square.* She has an extensive stage background and loves doing Shakespeare. Her distinctive voice and delightful accents (British upper class and cockney; Yiddish) are hallmarks of her performances. In her spare time she creates books on tape for the visually handicapped.

REDMOND STUDIOS

Lee's Cucumber Salad

(Serves 4 to 6)

2 medium cucumbers
2 cups yogurt
Garlic, to taste (minced or dried)
Dill weed, to taste, (chopped)
Parsley, to taste (fresh chopped or dried)
Chives, to taste (fresh chopped or freeze-dried)
Dash of lemon juice
Dijon mustard, to taste
Fresh ground black pepper, to taste

Wash and peel cucumbers, cut in half lengthwise and scoop out seeds. Slice cucumbers and mix with yogurt, garlic, dill, parsley, chives, lemon juice and pepper.

Variation

Two or three thinly sliced radishes may be added to the salad, but just before serving (to avoid turning the yogurt pink). In addition, or instead, sliced celery or fresh fennel may be added.

 =*Robert Mondavi Fumé Blanc*

BURGESS MEREDITH

Burgess Meredith was one of the most versatile and gifted actors of our century. Born in 1907, he started out as a merchant seaman and businessman. His remarkable performance in the 1936 stage production of *Winterset* won him instant acclaim and a trip to Hollywood to do the movie a year later. The younger generation will recognize him as The Penguin from the TV series "Batman" and as Grandpa in *Grumpy Old Men,* with Jack Lemmon and Walter Matthau, and *Grumpier Old Men,* starring the same men but with the added attraction of Sophia Loren. Mr. Meredith, twice nominated for an Academy Award, passed away during the preparation of this book. Movie lovers everywhere will miss him.

Meredith Malibu Nacho Salad

(Serves 4)

1 can (15 ounces) black beans
1 cup cooked or canned yellow corn kernels
1 cup cooked rice
1 onion, chopped
1 bunch of cilantro, leaves chopped
3 medium tomatoes, seeded and diced
Juice of 1 lime, or to taste
3 tablespoons olive oil
Salt and pepper, to taste
1 head lettuce
1 large bag tortilla chips
Grated cheese
Sour cream (optional)
Fresh salsa

Mix the beans, corn, rice, onion, cilantro, and tomatoes in a large bowl. In a small bowl, mix together the lime juice, olive oil, salt, and pepper. Use more or less lime juice as desired. Marinate the vegetables. Toss and serve on a bed of lettuce and tortilla chips. Top with grated cheese, sour cream, if desired, and fresh salsa.

=Robert Mondavi Winery Stag's Leap District Sauvignon Blanc

CRISTINA FERRARE

Cristina Ferrare is the host of television's "The Home & Family Show."

HOME & FAMILY

Arugula Salad with Black Olive and White Bean Crostini

(Serves 6)

Black Olive Spread

1 garlic clove, chopped
1 tablespoon extra virgin olive oil
1 cup drained and pitted European black olives, such as Gaeta, Kalamata, or Spanish, chopped.

White Bean Spread

1 can white beans or cannellini beans
Juice of 1 lemon
2 tablespoons olive oil
1 tablespoon chopped basil
Pinch of salt and pepper
12 to 18 slices French bread, toasted, for crostini

Vinaigrette

1 tablespoon white wine vinegar
1 tablespoon lemon juice
2 tablespoons walnut oil
Freshly ground black pepper

3 to 4 bunches of arugula (about 1½ pounds), trimmed, rinsed, and dried well
Chopped parsley, for garnish

 *=Robert Mondavi Winery Zinfandel*

For the black olive spread, put the garlic, olive oil, and olives in a food processor and chop until fine. Set aside. For the white bean spread, put all the ingredients in a food processor and mash to a coarse purée. Set aside. Spread half the crostini with the olive spread and half with the bean spread. Set aside.

Mix together all the ingredients for the vinaigrette. Put the arugula in a large bowl, pour on the vinaigrette, and toss well. Divide among 6 salad plates. Put 2 or 3 crostini on top of each salad or on the side of the plate. Sprinkle with chopped parsley and serve.

 =*Robert Mondavi Winery Zinfand*

Entrées

ELIZABETH TAYLOR

Elizabeth Taylor is a national treasure. From her childhood career, beginning with *There's One Born Every Minute* at age ten, to her Oscars for *Butterfield 8* and *Who's Afraid of Virginia Woolf*, Ms. Taylor has become famous with all generations. She is considered by many to be the most beautiful woman in the world, her unique violet eyes accenting her incredible beauty. She is active in AIDS research, having been the founding chairperson of AmFAR (American Foundation for AIDS Research) and the Elizabeth Taylor AIDS Foundation.

With much love,
Elizabeth Taylor

FIROOZ ZAHEDI © 1996

Spicy Chicken

(Serves 4 to 6)

2 teaspoons curry powder
1 teaspoon ground cumin
½ teaspoon ground ginger
½ teaspon turmeric
½ garlic clove, crushed
1 onion, chopped
1 teaspoon grated fresh ginger
1 medium chicken (about 3 pounds), skinned and cut into serving pieces

Combine the spices with the garlic, onion, and fresh ginger. Coat the chicken with this mixture and refrigerate for at least 2 hours, preferably longer. Place on a moderately hot barbecue grill or broil for about 30 minutes, or until done, turning once.

 =*Robert Mondavi Winery Coastal Chardonnay*

BARBARA EDEN

Barbara Eden will always be remembered as Jeannie in the Sixties TV series "I Dream of Jeannie" with Larry Hagman, her astronaut "master," who was never certain who was in charge. Barbara has appeared in several well-known films, including *Harper Valley P.T.A.*, *7 Faces of Dr. Lao*, and *Voyage to the Bottom of the Sea*. More recently, she made a number of highly rated TV movies. Barbara is active in charitable endeavors and received an honorary law degree from the University of West Los Angeles in 1990. Her mother gave her the recipe for Chicken Curry Casserole.

BARBARA EDEN

Barbara Eden

Chicken Curry Casserole

(Serves 8 to 10)

Step 1

2 whole chicken fryers or 4 to 5 bone-in chicken breasts
1 onion, sliced
1 tablespoon curry powder, or more to taste

Put the above ingredients in a large pot and cover with water. Cook until done, 25 to 30 minutes.

Step 2

1 small box long-grain rice

Cook rice according to directions on the box, using the broth from the chicken as liquid.

Step 3

Cooked chicken
Cooked rice
1 cup cream of mushroom soup
½ cup sour cream

Cut the chicken into bite-size pieces, add rice, cream of mushroom soup, and sour cream. Mix together and put in a covered dish. Bake at 350 degrees for 30 to 40 minutes.

 *= Woodbridge Chardonnay*

BOB HOPE

Bob Hope is one of the most famous and most loved entertainers of all time. His sense of humor and comic timing is unparalleled. His vaudeville background never really left his act, which evokes an earlier, more refined era yet provides us with timeless comedy. Mr. Hope has long shown his gratitude to his audiences and to his country; he entertained troops in World War II, and in the Korean, Vietnam, and Persian Gulf wars, always with beautiful women and great jokes that left everybody feeling better, even in the worst of times. Now he contributes a recipe to our book, showing his compassion and gratitude to people in need, as he did for our troops defending our freedom. Mr. Hope has been honored by the Academy of Motion Picture Arts & Sciences with five awards and was knighted by Queen Elizabeth II (Knight Commander of Most Excellent Order of the British Empire).

BOB HOPE ENTERPRISES

Favorite Chicken Hash

(Serves 4 to 6)

2 boneless, skinless chicken breasts, broiled
2 strips of bacon, fried until crisp
½ small onion, sautéed
2 tablespoons butter
½ teaspoon lemon juice
1 teaspoon dry sherry
Salt & pepper, to taste
2 tablespoons sour cream

Cut the chicken into fine strips. Crumble the bacon and combine with the onion, butter, lemon juice, salt, and pepper. Sauté in the butter until thoroughly heated. Shortly before serving, add the sherry and sour cream. Do not allow to cook after adding the last 2 ingredients, just heat through.

Love is like hash. You have to have confidence in it to enjoy it.
—Bob Hope as Huckleberry Hanes
in Jerome Kern's *Roberta,* 1933

 =*Woodbridge Chardonnay*

PHYLLIS DILLER

MARC RABOY

I was born under the "Sign of the Stomach," Cancer, and have had an avid interest in food all my life. Before I became a comic, as the mother of five children, I cooked for seven every day on a shoestring. They became tired of shoestrings and suggested I get to work and buy some pasta. The rest is history.

☆

Phyllis Diller is a comedienne who beat the odds when she made her sensational comedy debut in San Francisco and went on to become popular nationwide. She was nearly forty and a mother of five. She had a robust delivery and many of her jokes were at the expense of her first husband, "Fang." Ms. Diller's movies include *Happily Ever After,* and *Boy Did I Get a Wrong Number!* She keeps busy with her stand-up appearances.

Phyllis Diller's Chicken Charisma

(Serves 12)

6 boneless, skinless chicken breasts
Lots of butter
4 ounces mushrooms, sliced about ¼ inch thick
3 small cans or 2 large cans artichoke hearts, drained
3 tablespoons all-purpose flour
4 cups chicken stock or broth
1 can (15 ounces) chicken gravy (optional)
Salt and pepper, to taste
White wine

Sauté the chicken breasts in butter until brown. Remove from the pan and put in a baking dish. Add the mushrooms to the skillet and add more butter. Sauté the mushrooms. Sprinkle the mushrooms over the chicken in the baking dish. Arrange the artichokes artistically with the chicken in the baking dish, allowing 2 hearts per person. Add flour to the drippings in the skillet where you sautéed the mushrooms. Add chicken stock to make gravy. Make about 4 cups of gravy; if you don't have enough drippings for this, add the canned chicken gravy. Add salt and pepper. Add no garlic. Add white wine to taste. Pour the gravy over the entire casserole. Cover and bake at 350 degrees for about 1 hour, or until the chicken breasts are tender. Uncover the casserole for the last 15 minutes of baking.

= *Robert Mondavi Winery Napa Valley Chardonnay*

NICHELLE NICHOLS

Aboard the Starship Enterprise, on our five-year mission where no man or woman had gone before, we relied on scientifically advanced food production and preparation, which not only boosted our immune systems dramatically but even tasted good! Today, here on earth, the trend toward a healthier diet strives to achieve this futuristic goal by relying heavily on the Triple Fs: fruits, fish, and fowl. Within these pages you will find a myriad of culinary delights which I am sure will be enjoyed into the twenty-third century. But don't wait until then. Enjoy them now—and you will live long and prosper!

☆

Nichelle was discovered onstage by Duke Ellington and was hired on the spot as a singer with his band. That sky was not the limit for Nichelle; she went on to become Lieutenant Uhura of the Starship Enterprise in Gene Roddenberry's "Star Trek" series and lived in the hearts of all trekkies from then on. Nichelle got her star on the Hollywood Walk of Fame in January 1992. She received an honorary Doctor of Arts degree from Marywood College in 1995 and has received NASA's Distinguished Public Service Award. At home onstage, in the studio, or on the TV set, Nichelle is part of our most romantic dreams and adventures.

NICHELLE NICHOLS

Scallop Stir-fry

(Serves 4)

1 tablespoon sesame oil
1 tablespoon olive oil
1 pound bay scallops
1 tablespoon minced garlic
2 tablespoons minced ginger
1 can (8 ounces) button mushrooms, drained
1 can (8 ounces) baby corn, drained
1 can (8 ounces) sliced water chestnuts, drained (optional)
1 cup snow peas, fresh or frozen
4 scallions, cut into 1-inch pieces
1 red bell pepper, seeded and sliced
2 carrots, julienned
½ cup chicken stock
¼ cup dry sherry
2 tablespoons soy sauce
1 tablespoon cornstarch
Hot cooked white rice, for serving

Heat the sesame oil and olive oil in a skillet and sauté the scallops for 2 minutes, stirring constantly. Add the garlic, ginger, mushrooms, corn, water chestnuts, snow peas, scallions, bell pepper, and carrots. Sauté for 4 to 5 minutes more, or until tender. Combine the chicken stock, sherry, soy sauce, and cornstarch in a small bowl and mix well. Pour over the scallop mixture and cook 1 to 2 minutes, or until thickened. Serve with cooked white rice.

 =Vichon Chevrignon

ELIZABETH HURLEY

Elizabeth Hurley began her career as an actress before becoming a successful model for Estée Lauder and a producer for Simian Films. As an actress, Elizabeth's recent credits include *Permanent Midnight* with Ben Stiller and *Austin Powers: International Man of Mystery* with Mike Myers, and she will soon appear in the forthcoming feature films *Ed TV* with Matthew McConaughey and Disney's *My Favorite Martian*. Elizabeth has developed and produced two feature films, the romantic comedy *Mickey Blue Eyes* starring Hugh Grant, Jeanne Tripplehorn, and James Caan, and *Extreme Measures*, starring Hugh Grant and Gene Hackman.

ALBERT WATSON

Elizabeth Hurley

This is my all-time favorite recipe, taught to me by my father, although he uses beef instead of lamb, which of course you could do too. I don't really measure or weigh anything when I make this, so feel free to use more or less of most things, like carrots and onions. This is even better if you make the meat part a day early and refrigerate it overnight. Mash the potatoes the next day, slap them on top of the cold meat, and bake it in a 350-degree oven for about 45 minutes. I usually serve the pie with a large green salad.

Shepherd's Pie

(Serves 6 to 8)

3 tablespoons olive oil
1 large onion, chopped
4 large carrots, diced
2 pounds ground lamb
½ to 1 cup red wine
1 pint soup stock—lamb, chicken, or vegetable
2 sprigs of rosemary
Tomato paste in a tube
Salt and freshly ground black pepper, to taste
4 pounds potatoes, peeled and cut into chunks
Butter
Milk

Heat the olive oil in a skillet and fry the onion until soft. Add the carrots and cook for 5 minutes more. Add the lamb, quickly stirring with a wooden spoon so that most of the meat gets seared. Pour the wine over the meat. You choose how much; I normally use a wine glass or two. This will make everything start to sizzle so keep stirring. Add the rosemary, a squirt of tomato paste, a good pinch of salt, and some pepper. Add about half of the stock to the skillet. Stir it in and turn the heat down low. Keep an eye on it for the next 30 minutes as it cooks, adding more stock when necessary. The ideal consistency should be rich, moist, and glossy with no more than a few teaspoons of liquid. Keep tasting as it cooks and add more salt and pepper if you think they are needed.

Meanwhile boil the potatoes in plenty of salted water until soft. Drain thoroughly, then mash them ferociously with a large knob of butter, a good splash of milk, and plenty of black pepper.

Transfer the meat when it's ready into an ovenproof dish and spoon the mashed potatoes on top of it. Make furrows in the top of the potato with a fork. Put the dish at the top of a hot oven for 5 minutes or so, until the top is brown and crispy.

 *= Robert Mondavi Winery Napa Valley Pinot Noir*

ROBIN LEACH

ROBIN LEACH

Work hard, believe in yourself, and you will win. Be dedicated, diligent, and never give up on your dreams. It's a philosophy that works as well in life as in the kitchen. The first time I ever cooked a meal I burned my apartment building down. The next day I took cooking lessons, and I've never repeated the initial mistake! Always have friends celebrate good food and wonderful wines in the kitchen while you're preparing their meal. Champagne wishes and caviar dreams!

☆

A native of the United Kingdom, Robin Leach debated whether to seek his journalistic fortune in the United States or Australia. The United States won, and so did he with "Lifestyles of the Rich and Famous."

Silver and Gold Chicken

(Serves 4 to 6)

¼ pound (1 stick) unsalted butter
3 tablespoons all-purpose flour
2 cups Essence of Silver and Gold (recipe follows)
Salt and pepper, to taste
2 large onions, sliced
1 chicken (3 ½ to 5 pounds), cut into 8 pieces
1 cup Crystal champagne, or your favorite kind
¼ cup chopped fresh basil leaves, or 2 tablespoons dried basil
2 tablespoons chopped fresh oregano, or 1 tablespoon dried oregano
½ teaspoon dried mustard
1 tablespoon lemon juice
2 teaspoons Worcestershire sauce
8 ounces mushrooms, trimmed, washed, dried, and thinly sliced
1 pound carrots, halved and cut into 1-inch pieces
1 cup peas, fresh (about 1½ pounds unshelled) or frozen
4 medium potatoes (about 2 pounds), peeled and cut into ½-inch cubes
1 cup heavy cream, reduced to ½ cup

This recipe can be done in a clay pot designed for kitchen use, in a covered baking dish, or in a Dutch oven. If using a clay pot, soak it in cold water for 20 minutes before using and preheat the oven to 425 degrees. If using a baking dish or Dutch oven, preheat to 475 degrees.

Melt 3 tablespoons of the butter in a medium-size heavy saucepan over medium-high heat. Stir in the flour. Reduce the heat to medium and cook, whisking constantly, until well blended and the raw flavor of flour has dissipated, 3 to 5 minutes. Pour in the Essence of Silver and Gold and bring to a boil. Reduce the heat and simmer until thickened and smooth, 7 to 10 minutes. Stir often. Season with salt and pepper. Remove the sauce from the heat and keep warm.

Place the onions in the bottom of the clay pot or baking dish. Cut half of the remaining butter into thin slices and distribute evenly over the onions. Rinse the chicken and pat dry. Season with salt and pepper. Place the chicken on top of the onions and sprinkle with 3 tablespoons of the champagne. Add the basil, oregano, mustard, lemon juice, and Worcestershire. Arrange the mushrooms and the carrots on top of the chicken. Add the peas. Top with thin slices of the remaining butter. Sprinkle with 3 more tablespoons of champagne. Pour over the sauce and sprinkle with the remaining champagne. Sink the potato cubes into the sauce, leaving them slightly submerged. Cover tightly and bake until the vegetables are soft and chicken is done, about 45 to 50 minutes.

Remove the cover and cook until the protruding bits of potatoes are lightly browned, about 10 minutes more. Arrange the chicken and vegetables on a serving platter. Cover to keep warm. Add the reduced cream to the pan juices and boil for several minutes to reduce and thicken slightly. Pour over the chicken and serve immediately.

 = Robert Mondavi Winery Napa Valley Pinot Noir

Essence of Silver and Gold

(Makes 2 cups)

1 piece (1 pound) lean veal, cut from the leg
1 whole bone-in chicken breast (about 1 pound)
2 pounds veal bones, sawed into 4 to 5 pieces
1 leek, trimmed, washed, and coarsely chopped
1 stalk celery, thickly sliced
1 medium carrot, halved and thickly sliced
1 to 2 sprigs of fresh thyme or 1 teaspoon dried thyme
1 bay leaf
1 large onion stuck with 2 whole cloves
1 teaspoon salt
10 whole black peppercorns
2 cups good-quality dry white wine

Trim the veal and chicken of any fat. Combine all of the ingredients in a large stockpot. Pour over 6 cups of water. Bring to a boil over medium-high heat. Reduce the heat to medium and simmer, uncovered, until the liquid measures about 2 cups, 2 to 3 hours. Skim off any foam that rises to the top from time to time.

Line a large sieve or colander with a double layer of cheesecloth and set inside a large bowl. Carefully ladle in the hot stock. Discard the solids. Cool to room temperature, cover, and refrigerate. Remove any fat that hardens on top.

Tip: Use your best wine for this sauce. Spare not and the results will pay off in praise.

ISADORA ALMAN

It will come as no surprise that a woman whose life's work is sex and relationships would also love food. Browsing through my recipe collection or planning a dinner party is far more stimulating to me than reading standard erotica. The pleasures of the flesh are, well, the pleasures of the flesh. Taking a date to dinner is a traditional courtship maneuver; "The way to a man's heart is through his stomach," a traditional piece of folk wisdom. Often nothing can beat the basics—Mom's meatloaf or a heaping plate of buttery mashed potatoes. But as the palate becomes more sophisticated, some prefer more complex mélanges combining familiarity and surprise—like the delight of longtime lovers who know each other's bodies well yet still remain creative. Whatever your taste, I entreat you to revel in the pleasure. Enjoy yourself with the recipes here . . . and enjoy someone else as well!

LORI EANES

Isadora Alman

Isadora's Sweet and Sour Chicken

(Serves 4)

1 medium onion, sliced
2 tablespoons olive oil
6 pieces of chicken, skinned
1 teaspoon dried oregano
¼ teaspoon celery salt
Pepper
1 small can tomato sauce
½ cup red wine or sherry
1 tablespoon orange marmalade

Sauté the onion in the olive oil. Remove from the pan and brown the chicken pieces. Combine the browned chicken, onion, oregano, celery salt, pepper, tomato sauce, wine, and marmalade. Cook, covered, for 30 minutes, then uncovered until the sauce is at desired thickness.

Isadora Alman is a popular TV and radio talk show guest. She writes an advice column, "Ask Isadora," on sex and relationships. Isadora is an accomplished writer, speaker, and licensed counselor.

 = Woodbridge Zinfandel

MARIETTE HARTLEY

Emmy Award winner (six times nominated) and three-time Clio Award winner Mariette Hartley has established herself as an enduring star. She hosted "The CBS Morning Show" in 1987 and has appeared in more than a dozen feature films, including Sam Peckinpah's classic, *Ride the High Country*, Alfred Hitchcock's *Marnie*, *Skyjacked*, and *Improper Channels*. She has appeared in four television series, including "Peyton Place," TV's first prime-time soap opera; and "The Rockford Files.".

☆

A dish originally from Normandy: My mother-in-law served this in her Norman farmhouse.

CESARE BONAZZA

Mariette Hartley

Spaghetti Boyriven

(Serves 4 to 6)

1 pound bacon, smoked or regular, cut into ⅛-inch strips
1 tablespoon fresh thyme leaves
1 tablespoon crushed rosemary leaves
Black pepper, to taste
2 bay leaves
1 small can plain pitted green olives, drained and chopped
1 small can pitted black olives, drained and chopped
⅓ cup olive oil
4 garlic cloves, chopped
2 pounds spaghetti
Handful of cilantro leaves, chopped
Salt, to taste
½ cup grated romano, Swiss, or parmesan cheese
3 eggs

Put the bacon in a frying pan over medium heat and add the thyme, rosemary, black pepper, and one of the bay leaves. Let simmer, covered, until the bacon is medium-done. Do not pour off the bacon fat.

Add the green and black olives. Add the olive oil and garlic. Reduce the heat.

Fill a large pot with water and add salt and the remaining bay leaf. Bring to a boil, add the spaghetti, and cook until al dente. Add the cilantro to the bacon mixture. Do not let the mixture cook too long; the cilantro should retain its color and flavor. Drain the pasta and rinse. Put the pasta back into the pot and add the bacon mixture. Add the cheese and stir. Let cool down somewhat.

Just before serving, beat the eggs, pour over, and blend it all together. Stir and serve.

 *=Woodbridge Zinfandel*

DOM DELUISE

Unlike President Bush, I really love broccoli. I love it up or down or in a tree. I like it hot, I like it cold, I'm going to like it when I get old. And if it's just too mushy to eat, I'll blend it into a soup that can't be beat! Parboiled it's good in any salad with chicken or fish or in a ballad. When I see broccoli, I eat it raw. When I see broccoli, I just want more! The End.

☆

Talented character actor of stage, television, and film, Dom DeLuise has been entertaining audiences for more than thirty years. Some of his film and television credits include *Blazing Saddles, Silent Movie, Smokey and the Bandit, Cannonball Run* and *Cannonball Run II, The Best Little Whorehouse in Texas,* "The Dom DeLuise Show," and the new "Candid Camera." Dom is also an author and a superb chef.

DOM DELUISE

Broccoli with Rigatoni

(Serves 4)

½ cup olive oil
2 tablespoons butter
4 garlic cloves, minced
1 bunch of broccoli, separated into florets
1 cup chicken stock
Salt, to taste
1 pound rigatoni
1 cup fresh basil leaves, coarsely chopped
Chopped parsley
Coarsely ground black pepper
½ cup grated parmesan cheese

Heat the oil and butter in a large skillet over low heat, add the garlic, and gently brown it. Add the broccoli and stir gently until it turns bright green. Add the broth, cover, and simmer until the broccoli is al dente. Add half the basil and set aside.

Put a large pot of water on to boil. Add salt. Add the rigatoni and cook, uncovered, until done. Drain the rigatoni, add it to the broccoli, and mix thoroughly. Transfer to a hot serving dish, sprinkle with parsley, pepper, grated cheese, and the remaining basil and serve.

 =*Robert Mondavi Winery Coastal Chardonnay*

MIKE BURGER

Popular, homemaker-friendly co-host (with Cristina Ferrare) of "The Home & Family Show," Mike Burger loves to cook. To see him cook in person, tune in to the show.

HOME & FAMILY

Michael Burger

Mike's Lucky Chicken

(Serves 4)

½ cup all-purpose flour
1 teaspoon salt
1 pound boneless, skinless chicken breast, cut into bite-size pieces
2 tablespoons vegetable oil
1 tablespoon butter
½ cup chopped celery
½ cup chopped red bell pepper
½ cup chopped green bell pepper
½ cup chopped onion
2 tablespoons brown sugar
½ teaspoon pepper
1 cup catsup
Hot cooked brown rice, for serving

Combine the flour and salt and roll the chicken in the mixture to coat. Heat the oil and butter in a wok or skillet, add the chicken, and cook until browned on all sides. Combine all the other ingredients, except the rice, in a bowl, and pour over the chicken. Cover and simmer for 30 minutes, or until the vegetables are tender. Serve with brown rice.

 =Robert Mondavi Winery Coastal Pinot Noir

CARNIE WILSON

I am so happy to be part of this cookbook. I love to cook, but more important— this cause is so very worthy. I hope we can make a difference. Love and kisses— and good food!!

☆

Carnie Wilson teamed up with her sister Wendy and friend Chynna Phillips (daughter of Michelle Phillips) to create Wilson Phillips, one of the hottest groups of the Nineties. Their debut album contained four top-five hit singles, three of which hit number one. The group sold nearly twelve million albums in their first two years. Carnie's love of music started very early in life when she sang at the piano with her father, the legendary Beach Boy Brian Wilson.

CARNIE WILSON

Love and kisses (and good food!)

Carnie Wilson

♡

Fettuccine with Chicken

(Serves 4)

2 tablespoons olive oil
4 boneless, skinless chicken breasts, cut into 1-inch-thick strips
1 teaspoon chopped oregano
1 teaspoon chopped basil
1 teaspoon chopped parsley
¼ teaspoon celery salt
2 garlic cloves, minced
Freshly ground black pepper, to taste
1 red bell pepper, seeded and chopped
1 pound fettuccine
¼ pound (1 stick) butter or margarine
½ cup heavy cream
1 cup grated parmesan cheese

Heat the olive oil in a sauté pan over medium heat. Add the chicken, oregano, basil, parsley, celery salt, garlic, and black pepper. Cook for 5 minutes. Add the red pepper and continue to cook for 3 to 4 minutes, or until the chicken is cooked through. Remove the chicken and peppers from the pan and set aside.

Fill a large pot with water, add salt, and bring to a boil. Add the fettuccine, and cook until al dente. Drain. Melt the butter in a saucepan over low heat. Add the pasta, cream, parmesan cheese, chicken, and peppers. Heat through and serve.

=Robert Mondavi Winery Napa Valley Chardonnay or Pinot Noir

CCH POUNDER

Emmy-nominated CCH Pounder has had a colorful life. She has appeared in more than a dozen films and more than two dozen TV shows and has an extensive theater background. She grew up on a sugar plantation in Guyana, attended school in England, and went to college in the United States. She is currently known for her role as Dr. Angela Hicks on the highly rated TV series "ER."

CCH POUNDER

Paul
Best of luck with your
wonderful idea for
great recipes!

all the best
CCH Pounder

Charmaine Lewis's Fish Escabeche
with Fruity Salsa

(Serves 2, or one hearty eater)

Vegetable oil, for frying
1 pound whole snapper, cleaned; the squeamish can remove the head
½ cup flour, seasoned with salt, pepper, and curry powder, for dredging
½ cup rice vinegar, preferably plain
½ Scotch bonnet (habanero) chili pepper or 1 jalapeño, finely diced while wearing gloves
1 medium onion, sliced and separated into rings
1 teaspoon brown sugar (optional)
Thinly sliced red cabbage, for serving
Cooked rice, for serving
Fruity Salsa (recipe follows)
Plain water crackers, for serving

Heat enough oil to cover the fish entirely. Dredge the fish in flour and fry it in the hot oil in a frying pan large enough to hold the fish, for about 5 minutes, being careful not to overcook. Drain well and keep warm in a glass or ceramic dish. Combine the vinegar, chili pepper, and onion in a small saucepan and bring to a boil. If the mixture is too tart, stir in the brown sugar. Pour the vinegar mixture over the fish. Let the fish stand for 1 hour to absorb the flavors.

Arrange the fish on a bed of thinly sliced red cabbage and cooked rice. Serve with salsa.

Fruity Salsa

(Makes ½ cup)

Mix together 2 tablespoons *each* finely diced pineapple, papaya, and yellow bell pepper, and canned black beans (drained). Season with salt, pepper, and 1 tablespoon dried cilantro. This dish tastes good with crackers. It tastes even better the next day.

 = Woodbridge White Zinfandel

RITA MORENO

Dancer par excellence, star of stage, screen, and TV, Rita is the only female performer to have won the Grand Slam—all four of the most prestigious show business awards. She won the Oscar in 1961, the Grammy in 1973, the Tony in 1975, and the Emmy, twice, in 1977 and 1978. Rita's energy remains the same, from *West Side Story* to the many benefits she does now for worthy causes.

RITA MORENO

Beef Picadillo

(Serves 6)

¼ cup annatto oil
1 large onion, finely chopped
1 garlic clove, finely chopped
1 large green bell pepper, seeded and finely chopped
1 fresh hot red or green chili pepper, seeded and chopped
2 pounds ground round steak
2 large tomatoes, peeled and chopped
½ teaspoon ground cumin
Salt and freshly ground black pepper, to taste
½ cup seedless raisins
¼ cup pimiento-stuffed green olives, chopped
1 tablespoon capers, rinsed and drained

FOR SERVING
Cooked white rice
Black beans
Fried plantains

Heat the oil in a large frying pan and cook the onion, garlic, bell pepper, and hot pepper until the onion is tender but not browned. Add the meat and cook, stirring and breaking it up until it has lost its color. Add the tomatoes, cumin, salt, and pepper. Add the raisins, mix thoroughly, and simmer gently, uncovered, until cooked, about 20 minutes. Add the olives and capers and cook for a few minutes longer. Serve with rice, black beans, and fried plantains.

=*Robert Mondavi Winery Carneros District Pinot Noir*

JANE LEEVES

Jane, a native of the United Kingdom, plays the vivacious Daphne Moon, heartthrob of Niles Crane on the popular TV series "Frasier."

JANE LEEVES

Shepherd's Pie with Beef

(Serves 4)

2 pounds potatoes, peeled and cut into chunks
3 tablespoons milk
2 tablespoons butter
Salt and pepper, to taste
1 tablespoon vegetable oil
1 large onion, chopped
1 pound ground beef
½ cup beef stock
1 carrot, diced
1 cup frozen peas
1 tablespoon Worcestershire sauce
1 tablespoon flour

Cook the potatoes in boiling salted water for 15 to 20 minutes, then drain and mash with milk, butter, and salt and pepper. Set aside.

Heat the oil in a frying pan, add the onion, and fry for about 5 minutes. Stir in the ground beef, stock, carrot, peas, Worcestershire, and salt and pepper. Add the flour and cook to thicken. Heat until simmering. Spoon the meat into an ovenproof dish, cover with the mashed potatoes, and mark the top with a fork. Bake at 375 degrees for 25 to 30 minutes. Brown at the end of cooking under the broiler until the top is crispy golden brown.

=*Robert Mondavi Winery Coastal Cabernet Sauvignon*

CHEVY CHASE

Chevy is one of the most popular comedians of our time. He became famous as a regular on "Saturday Night Live," went on to star with Beverly D'Angelo as the Griswolds in the hilarious *National Lampoon's Vacation* series, and has starred in several other popular movies, notably, Neil Simon's *Seems Like Old Times* and *Foul Play*, with Goldie Hawn and Burgess Meredith. This recipe is from Chevy's wife, Jayni.

CHEVY CHASE

Vegetable Lasagna

(Serves 8)

1 box curly edge lasagna noodles
2 pounds broccoli, chopped
2 teaspoons oil
4 medium zucchini, chopped
1 medium onion, chopped
2 garlic cloves, minced
1 can (28 ounces) whole tomatoes
3 cups skim milk ricotta cheese
¾ pound mozzarella cheese
½ cup grated parmesan cheese
1 teaspoon dried oregano
1 can (16 ounces) spaghetti sauce

Preheat oven to 350 degrees. Cook the lasagna noodles as directed on the box. Steam the broccoli for 2 minutes. Heat the oil in a frying pan and fry the broccoli, zucchini, onion, garlic, tomatoes, and salt for about 5 minutes over high heat. In a large bowl, combine the ricotta, mozzarella, parmesan, and oregano. Mix well. Warm the spaghetti sauce in a saucepan.

Spread half of the spaghetti sauce on the bottom of a 13 × 9-inch baking dish. Place a layer of lasagna noodles over the sauce, then spread a layer of the tomato-vegetable mixture. Add a layer of the cheese mixture. Top that with a layer of lasagna noodles. Repeat layers, ending with lasagna. Top with the other half of the spaghetti sauce. Bake for 45 minutes.

= Robert Mondavi Winery Merlot

JAMES EARL JONES

James Earl Jones, a formidable actor, has worked steadily in theater to considerable acclaim. In 1969 he won a Tony for the stage performance of Jack Jefferson in *The Great White Hope*. In 1970 he was nominated for an Academy Award and won a Golden Globe for the same role in the film version. He won another Tony in 1987 for a powerful performance in August Wilson's *Fences*. Mr. Jones has conquered all realms of acting from Hollywood to Broadway with his great range of roles, from Shakespeare to Star Wars. Other films include *Dr. Strangelove, Exorcist II: The Heretic, Field of Dreams,* and *Cry, the Beloved Country.* His distinctive voice is often heard in radio and TV announcements.

JAMES EARL JONES

Chilean Sea Bass

(Serves 6)

10 Maui onions, sliced
5 shallots, chopped
¼ pound (1 stick) unsalted butter
12 (fresh or canned) plum tomatoes, seeded and chopped
3 garlic cloves, minced
3 basil leaves, chopped
1 tablespoon extra virgin olive oil
½ cup chicken broth
12 pieces Chilean sea bass, 2½ × 2 inches
Salt and white pepper, to taste

Cook the onions and shallots in a skillet on low heat until caramelized, 1 to 2 hours. Set aside. Puree the butter, tomatoes, garlic, and basil. Heat the olive oil. Add the butter mixture and cook on low heat for 30 minutes. Add chicken broth as necessary.

Season the bass with salt and white pepper. Cover the bass with the onion mixture. Bake at 425 degrees for 10 to 12 minutes. Divide among 6 dinner plates and pour sauce over each.

= *Robert Mondavi Winery Carneros District Chardonnay*

CORLISS TILLMAN

Corliss Tillman is founder and president of Professional Women in Business, a professional development company. She is also a motivational speaker. Ms. Tillman has coached individuals on career dilemmas and how to realize their dreams and goals. Over the years she has earned the respect of her peers as someone who has excelled as a savvy businesswoman. She is the author of *Repackage Yourself: Success Strategies for Your Career, Business and Life.*

Shrimp Gumbo

(Serves 4 to 6)

3½ tablespoons vegetable oil
2 tablespoons flour
1 pound raw shrimp, peeled and deveined
1 cup chopped celery
2 onions, chopped
1¼ pounds fresh okra, sliced
1 can (14½ ounces) tomatoes, with juice
2 bay leaves
Salt and pepper, to taste
1 can (6 ounces) tomato paste
3 cups hot cooked rice

Heat 2 tablespoons of the vegetable oil in a medium skillet. Add the flour and stir constantly until rich dark brown. Stir in the shrimps and cook for a few minutes.

Heat the remaining 1½ tablespoons oil in a large saucepan over medium heat. Add the celery and onions and cook until soft and transparent. Add the okra and cook for about 30 minutes. Add the tomatoes, 3 cups water, bay leaves, salt, and pepper. Stir in the shrimp mixture, cover, and simmer for 15 minutes. Add the tomato paste and cook for 15 minutes more.

Remove the bay leaves before serving. Serve in shallow bowls over rice.

 =*Robert Mondavi Winery Napa Valley Zinfandel*

BARBARA BUSH

Barbara Bush, the enormously popular former First Lady, is sensible and down to earth. While fulfilling her official duties, she also crusaded against illiteracy and supported programs to fight drug abuse and help the homeless. She now volunteers her time and efforts to conquer leukemia. She has written three books: *C. Fred's Story, Millie's Book,* and her autobiography, *Barbara Bush: A Memoir.* Mrs. Bush has also helped develop the Barbara Bush Foundation for Family Literacy.

WHITE HOUSE PHOTO

Barbara Bush

Barbecued Chicken

(Serves 4)

Marinade

1 chicken (about 3 pounds), quartered
1 large garlic clove, crushed; 1 teaspoon salt
½ teaspoon freshly ground black pepper
1 tablespoon oil; 3 tablespoons lemon juice

*P*ut the marinade ingredients in a heavy plastic bag with a zipper closure. Shake to coat well. Refrigerate for 24 hours if possible, turning the bag several times. When coals are ready, place chicken on the grill, skin side up, and baste with the marinade. Cook until well browned before turning. (If baking in oven, bake at 400 degrees, skin side down first.) About 20 minutes before the chicken is done, begin using your favorite bottled barbecue sauce or the following version.

Barbecue Sauce

¼ cup cider vinegar; 2 ¼ cups water; ¾ cup sugar
¼ pound (1 stick) butter or margarine
⅓ cup yellow mustard; 2 onions, coarsely chopped
½ teaspoon each salt and pepper

Bring the barbecue sauce ingredients along with 2½ cups water to a boil and cook on low heat for 20 minutes, or until the onion is tender. Then add:

¼ cup Worcestershire sauce
2½ cups catsup; 6 to 8 tablespoons lemon juice
Cayenne, to taste

Simmer slowly for 45 minutes. Taste for seasoning. (This sauce freezes well.)

=*Robert Mondavi Winery Coastal Pinot Noir*

DEBBIE REYNOLDS

At the age of sixteen, Debbie Reynolds won the Miss Burbank title and a Warner Brothers screen test. That put her on the fast track. In 1950 she starred with Fred Astaire in *Three Little Words* and in 1952 she was in the Hollywood classic *Singin' in the Rain* with Gene Kelly. In 1957 she scored a Number One record with her rendition of "Tammy" from the film *Tammy and the Bachelor*. She received an Academy Award nomination for her performance in the hit *The Unsinkable Molly Brown*. Ms. Reynolds continues performing today in nightclubs and concerts as well as starring in films and on television. You can catch her act in the renowned Debbie Reynolds Hotel & Casino in Las Vegas.

HARRY LANGDON

Eggplant Casserole

(Serves 4)

1 large eggplant
Salt
3 medium tomatoes, sliced
1 cup grated Swiss cheese
1 cup grated parmesan cheese
4 tablespoons (½ stick) butter
½ cup tomato sauce
1 cup seasoned bread crumbs
Salt and pepper, to taste

Peel and slice the eggplant. Soak it in cold salted water for about 30 minutes. Grease the bottom and sides of a 13 × 9-inch baking dish. Add a layer of eggplant slices and a layer of tomato slices. Sprinkle with a third of the Swiss and parmesan cheese. Repeat the procedure, ending with a layer of eggplant. Dot with butter and pour the tomato sauce on top. Cover with bread crumbs and top with the remaining cheese. Bake at 350 degrees for 1 hour.

 =Robert Mondavi Winery Napa Valley Zinfandel

JAYNE MEADOWS AND STEVE ALLEN

According to Jayne, "My favorite food is Chinese; it's delicious, imaginative, and healthy. I was born in Wuhan, China, on the banks of the Yangtze River. My favorite vegetable was Gno (pronounced like a nasal no), the roots of water lilies. I'd offer a small fortune for a taste of it today!"

☆

Jayne Meadows, actress and comedienne, is currently touring the world with her one-woman show. In addition to her many film credits, she has made many cameo appearances on TV shows.

Sir Noel Coward described Steve Allen as "the most talented man in America." He has written more than forty books, published sixty-eight hundred songs, and made over fifty-two record albums and CDs. Mr. Allen succeeded Milton Berle as the Abbot of the world-famous Friars Club. He was the creator and original host of the "Tonight Show" and he has been inducted into TV's Academy Hall of Fame. Steve Allen and Jayne Meadows have one of the most enduring marriages in Hollywood.

THE STEVE ALLEN OFFICE

love,
Jayne Meadows ★
Steve Allen

Shrimp Flambé Newburg

(Serves 4)

2 tablespoons butter
1 Spanish onion chopped
12 jumbo shrimp, peeled and deveined
2 jiggers brandy
1 cup heavy cream
1 egg yolk
1 teaspoon chopped parsley
Dash of cayenne
Salt, to taste
Rice pilaf, for serving

Melt the butter in a skillet over medium heat and sauté the onion until brown. Add the shrimp and cook for 10 minutes. Add the brandy and ignite it. Cook until the flame goes out.

Blend together the cream, egg yolk, parsley, and cayenne. Add to the shrimp mixture and stir well without letting the sauce thicken. Add salt to taste. Serve hot with pilaf.

 = *Robert Mondavi Winery Napa Valley Chardonnay*

CHARLES PEREZ

This is one of my favorite Peruvian dishes. It is called arroz tapado, literally "covered" or "stuffed rice." The dish is so named because the rice is molded around a meat filling, then unmolded on a plate. The presentation is as important as the recipe itself. It's yours to enjoy—a colorful and delicious taste of South America.

☆

Charles Perez was producer of "Montel Williams," "Ricki Lake," "Leeza," and "Jane Pratt." His production background uniquely qualifies him for his job as co-host of "American Journal." He constantly travels across the country, giving a series of motivational talks aimed toward young people at colleges and universities.

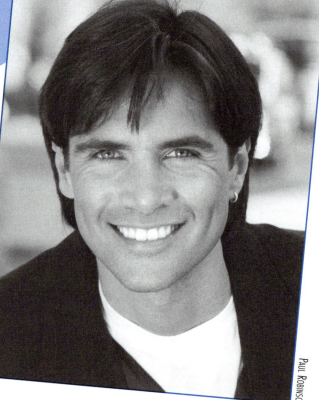

PAUL ROBINSON

Stuffed Rice

(Serves 4)

4 tablespoons olive oil
½ onion, chopped
½ red bell pepper, seeded and chopped
1¼ pounds ground sirloin
12 black olives, pitted and chopped
20 raisins
1 cup raw rice
Salt and pepper, to taste
4 sprigs of parsley, for garnish (optional)

Pour 2 tablespoons of the olive oil into a sauté pan over medium heat. Add the onions and red peppers and sauté until soft. Add the ground sirloin and sauté until brown. Add the olives, raisins, salt, and pepper, mix well, and set aside.

Bring 2 cups water to a boil in a medium saucepan and add salt and the remaining 2 tablespoons olive oil. Add the rice, reduce the heat to low, and simmer, covered, for about 15 minutes. Remove from the heat.

Place 3 to 4 tablespoons of cooked rice inside a teacup, pressing in firmly. Add some of the meat mixture, leaving a space at the top to cover the meat with rice. Add 2 tablespoons rice and press it down. Carefully place the cup upside down on a flat dish. Let stand for a few seconds, then lift off the cup. Continue until all the rice and meat are used. Garnish with a sprig of parsley on top, if desired.

= Robert Mondavi Winery Napa Valley Cabernet Sauvignon

MICHAEL FEINSTEIN

Spending most of my time on the road, I find that one of my favorite foods is pasta because of the energy I get from carbs. There is a long history of music and its relation to food, so to paraphrase Shakespeare, If music be the food of love, let's eat!

☆

Singer Michael Feinstein's many fine recordings and live performances are vibrant affairs! He has sold out shows at New York's Carnegie Hall, entertained at the White House, and performed on the Broadway stage. He has been nominated for a Grammy Award and has recorded more than a dozen albums. In 1977 he met and began working for Ira Gershwin. During the next six years he learned a great deal about interpreting song.

DAVID STOITZ

Michael Feinstein

Peppery Pasta

(Serves 6)

Sauce

3 pounds tomatoes, seeded and chopped
8 scallions, chopped
8 garlic cloves, minced
2 medium-size sweet banana peppers, sliced thin
½ cup chopped cilantro
¼ cup chopped basil
½ teaspoon salt

1 tablespoon olive oil
8 green bell peppers, seeded and chopped
3 yellow bell peppers, seeded and sliced thin
3 red bell peppers, seeded and sliced thin
1 teaspoon crushed red pepper
2 cups sliced white mushrooms
1 pound pasta, cooked
8 ounces mozzarella cheese, shredded

Combine the sauce ingredients in a saucepan and bring to a boil. Reduce the heat and simmer for 45 to 60 minutes.

Meanwhile, heat the olive oil in a large skillet, add the onions, sliced yellow and red bell peppers, crushed red pepper, and mushrooms. Sauté for 7 to 10 minutes, or until the vegetables are al dente. Place the cooked pasta on a serving platter. Pour the tomato sauce over the pasta, spoon the pepper-mushroom mixture over the sauce, and top with shredded mozzarella cheese. Serve immediately. *Mangia!*

=*Byron Santa Barbara Pinot Noir*

JANET LEIGH

Eat, drink, and be merry! This will certainly help in the eating department! And because of this book, people in need will be helped.

☆

Silver-screen star Norma Shearer saw a picture of Janet on the front desk of the ski resort where Janet's father worked and asked if she could borrow it. That led to a screen test at MGM and a leading role in *The Romance of Rosy Ridge*. She played in a number of films with stars including Errol Flynn, Gary Cooper, Judy Garland, and Jimmy Stewart. She went on to make a number of successful movies, including *Little Women, Angels in the Outfield, The Black Shield of Falworth, The Manchurian Candidate,* and many other Westerns, dramas, comedies, and musicals. Ms. Leigh has appeared in more than fifty films, but her most memorable was the small-budget movie *Psycho*, directed by Alfred Hitchcock. For her role in that film she was nominated for an Academy Award and won the Golden Globe.

JANET LEIGH

Enjoy!
Janet Leigh

Lamb Shanks

(Serves 1 to 2)

1 lamb shank, browned
1 onion, sliced
2 whole cloves
2 tablespoons brown sugar
2 tablespoons vinegar
Salt and pepper, to taste
Pinch of celery seed or celery salt
Chopped garlic, to taste
1 teaspoon ground ginger
Dash of Worcestershire sauce
½ cup red wine
1 can cream of mushroom soup
1 can cream of celery soup
3 tablespoons all-purpose flour (optional)

Combine all the ingredients except the flour in a roasting pan, cover, and braise for 6 to 7 hours on low heat. If a thicker gravy is desired, make a smooth paste with the flour and 3 tablespoons water, mix in, and cook for another 30 minutes or so. *Et voila!*

 = *Robert Mondavi Winery Napa Valley Cabernet Sauvignon*

REGIS PHILBIN

Regis Philbin is a TV personality and talk show host. He co-hosts "Live with Regis and Kathie Lee," a show that boasts an audience of eighteen million weekly. Mr. Philbin is a Notre Dame alumni and sports fanatic. This recipe was created by Regis's wife, Joy.

REGIS PHILBIN

Hope you like it

Regis

Joy's Pasta à la Passion

(Serves 4)

2 garlic cloves, minced
¼ cup extra virgin olive oil
¾ pound boneless, skinless chicken breast, cut into strips
2 cups broccoli florets
¾ cup oil-packed sun-dried tomatoes, drained and sliced thin
1 teaspoon dried basil
Pinch of crushed red pepper
Salt and pepper, to taste
¼ cup white wine
¾ cup chicken broth
1 to 2 tablespoons butter
8 ounces bow tie pasta, cooked
Freshly grated parmesan cheese (optional)

Sauté the garlic in the olive oil in a large skillet until golden. Add the chicken and sauté until cooked. Push the chicken to the side of the pan and add the broccoli. Sauté until the florets are crisp-tender. Add the sun-dried tomatoes, the basil, crushed red pepper, salt, pepper, wine, and broth. Add the butter, cover, and simmer for 5 minutes over low heat.

Remove from the heat and add the cooked pasta. Toss and serve with parmesan cheese, if desired.

=Byron Santa Barbara Pinot Noir

JOANNE WOODWARD

Joanne is one of
the most highly regarded
performers of the
American stage and
screen. Her movies include
Rachel, Rachel and *Three
Faces of Eve,* for which
she won the Academy
Award. (She was
nominated four times.)

JOANNE WOODWARD

Sole Cabernet

(Serves 4)

2 tablespoons melted butter
2 large shallots, chopped very fine
4 Dover sole fillets
Salt and pepper
1 tablespoon chopped basil
1 cup Cabernet Sauvignon
2 cups Hollandaise sauce

Put the melted butter and shallots in a shallow ovenproof pan and spread evenly. Arrange the fillets on top and sprinkle with salt and pepper and basil. Pour the wine over. Cover the pan and bake at 450 degrees for 10 minutes.

Remove the fillets and put on a serving platter. Reduce the liquid on top of stove to a fourth of original amount. Blend in the Hollandaise. Strain the sauce through a sieve and pour over the fillets. Serve immediately.

=*Robert Mondavi Winery Coastal Cabernet Sauvignon*

JANE RUSSELL

© WAIF

Anyone who knows me will laugh at the idea that I ever cooked, but this project touches the humanity in all of us. As founder of WAIF, I've been working on behalf of homeless children in need of loving, adoptive families for more than forty years. The children we help are older or have special needs—our work with children born drug addicted, suffering from fetal alcohol syndrome, or HIV-positive is the hardest but most rewarding of all we have accomplished. I'll always be remembered as the Howard Hughes pin-up or for the haystack photo that catapulted me to fame, but my work for children has helped more than forty-five thousand kids find adoptive families. This other career of mine is the very best work I've ever done!

Jane Russell

Pepper Steak à la Jane Russell

(Serves 6)

2 pounds trimmed top round, cut into ½-inch strips
2 tablespoons olive oil
2 to 4 garlic cloves, crushed
2 large green bell peppers, seeded and cut into thin strips
2 large onions, coarsely chopped
8 ounces mushrooms, sliced
½ teaspoon pepper
2 teaspoons salt
1 to 2 garlic cloves, finely chopped or pressed
¾ cup red wine
5 to 6 pinches of curry powder
Cooked white rice, for serving

Brown the meat in the olive oil in a heavy skillet with 1 to 2 cloves garlic. In another skillet, sauté the bell peppers and onions. When the vegetables are tender, add the mushrooms, pepper, salt, and the remaining garlic.

Add the vegetables to the browned beef. Add the wine and cook slowly for 30 minutes. Add the curry powder and simmer for 1 hour. Serve over cooked rice. This is great re-heated.

 =*Robert Mondavi Winery Napa Valley Zinfandel*

MICHELE LEE

WILLIAM DUSH

During her extraordinary performing career, Michele Lee has appeared on TV, Broadway, and the big screen. She is an accomplished recording artist and TV producer. As Karen MacKenzie in the CBS show "Knots Landing," Michele appeared in all 344 episodes. Her boundless energy carries her beyond her entertainment work to embrace a wide range of humanitarian causes. Michele enjoys a special quality rare in her industry—she cherishes her career, but her family comes first and her friendships run deep and are lasting.

Shrimp Pasta à la Zefferelli

(Serves 10)

3 pounds shrimp, peeled and deveined
Juice of 4 lemons
1 bunch of cilantro, leaves chopped
½ bunch of basil, leaves chopped
Pepper, to taste
2 onions, chopped
2 balls of mozzarella cheese, cubed or shredded
20 small tomatoes, seeded and chopped
2 stalks celery, chopped
2 pounds pasta, cooked

Boil the shrimp in salted water for 5 to 6 minutes. Drain. Combine the shrimp and all the other ingredients, except the pasta, in a large bowl and mix well. Pour the shrimp mixture over the hot pasta; the cheese will melt. (The shrimp-vegetable mixture keeps well in the refrigerator for several days. When ready to serve, just pour over hot pasta, any serving size.)

In 1976 Franco Zefferelli was in Los Angeles to direct a movie. He lived down the street and did not have a kitchen. Next to directing and the opera, he loved to cook more than anything else in the world. He spent every weekend in our kitchen whipping up Italian dishes for us. Everyone stood around the stove and watched the master at work. Italian pastas were his specialty. Eating Italian pastas was mine. This dish is one of my favorites.

 =*Vichon Napa Valley Chardonnay*

LIZ SMITH

I whomped up my original recipe for chicken-fried steak from memory and went to the New York apartment of my Texas pal Joe Armstrong to make up a batch for a cooking feature. He had a nice kitchen and I didn't, so we thought the photo of us cooking would look better taken in his apartment. I bought the meat, the milk, the eggs, the oil and arrived at Joe's. I hadn't bought the flour because every kitchen is equipped with such a staple. Lo and behold, Joe had never cooked anything in his divine kitchen, and he had no flour. The photographer was set up. It was night, and we were near Beekman Place with no grocery stores nearby. I said to Joe, "What are we going to do? We need flour to show in the photo. We are dredging the meat through it." Joe drawled, "Well, I have some Johnson & Johnson baby powder. It looks like flour." And so in the original photo taken of me cooking chicken-fried steak, the flour is baby powder. It looked fine. But we didn't get to eat any chicken-fried steak that night!

LIZ SMITH

Chicken-fried Steak

(Serves 6)

3 pounds round steak, sliced thin for frying (about ⅛ inch)
Black pepper, to taste
1 cup all-purpose flour, for dredging
4 eggs
Vegetable oil, for frying
Salt
1 tablespoon all-purpose or instant-dissolving flour, for gravy
Whole or skim milk or half-and-half, depending on how rich you want your gravy

Lay the steak on a flat surface and sprinkle with black pepper. Beat it on both sides with a mallet to tenderize it. Trim off any fat. Cut the meat into small pieces like veal piccata. Beat the eggs in a shallow bowl and spread out the flour on a flat plate. Heat the oil in a large frying pan until hot. Dip the meat in the egg, then in the flour, and place in the skillet. Fry fairly fast, turn, browning on both sides, and remove to paper towels. Sprinkle with salt.

Pour off the excess grease, leaving as much drippings as possible. Put the frying pan over medium heat, add 1 or 2 teaspoons flour, and stir into the drippings to thicken. (If you use instant-dissolving flour you can add more flour later if you like.) Fill up your gravy boat or pitcher with a mixture of milk and water. Gradually stir into the flour and drippings in the pan. Keep stirring the gravy and tasting—you need to season it with salt and pepper to taste as it cooks. Pepper and salt are the secret to flavor here. If the gravy becomes too thick, don't panic. Add more milk or water. Pour the gravy into the gravy boat or pitcher when it seems the right consistency to you. Serve instantly. If you have a candle warmer under it so much the better. This makes a terrific meal with biscuits and potatoes, tomato and lettuce salad or pineapple chunks and lettuce, Cheddar cheese bits, and mayonnaise. It is excellent cold and left over.

=*Robert Mondavi Winery Coastal Pinot Noir*

PETER RECKELL

In 1983 Peter Reckell joined the cast of "Days of Our Lives" as Bo Brady, the rugged cop. He also had a recurring role on the prime-time series "Knots Landing." Stage credits include *Jesus Christ Superstar, Guys & Dolls, Pirates of Penzance,* and *Death Trap.* In his spare time he enjoys practicing yoga and martial arts, swimming, and horseback riding.

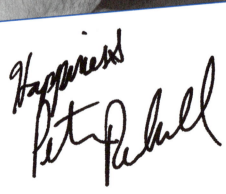

Chicken Vegetable Stir-fry

(Serves 4)

1 pound boneless, skinless chicken breast, cut into 1-inch cubes
2 tablespoons sherry
4 cups broccoli florets
2 tablespoons soy sauce
1 teaspoon chili paste (optional)
1 tablespoon cornstarch
1 tablespoon oil
1 cup julienned carrots
5 cups spinach
1 cup sliced mushrooms
Hot cooked rice, for serving

Marinate the chicken in the sherry for 30 minutes. Steam the broccoli for 2 to 3 minutes or until bright green, remove from the heat, and set aside. In a small cup combine soy sauce, ¼ cup water, chili paste, if using, and cornstarch. Heat the oil in a skillet or wok and sauté the chicken and carrots for 3 to 4 minutes. Add the soy-cornstarch mixture, spinach, and mushrooms and cook for 5 to 6 minutes. Serve over hot rice.

 =Robert Mondavi Winery Coastal Pinot Noir

MORGAN FAIRCHILD

MORGAN FAIRCHILD

Morgan Fairchild began her career on Broadway. She was later cast in the TV serial "Search for Tomorrow" before going to Hollywood, where she landed the part of Jenna Wade in "Dallas." Her first starring role was Constance Weldon Carlyle in the series "Flamingo Road." Later credits include Racine in "Paper Dolls," Jordan Roberts in "Falcon Crest," "Honeyboy," "North and South II," and *The Zany Adventures of Robin Hood.*

Pacific Red Snapper

(Serves 4)

4 red snappers (1 pound each), cleaned and scaled
¼ cup olive oil
12 garlic cloves
¼ teaspoon salt
¼ teaspoon pepper
1 teaspoon dried thyme leaves
1 tablespoon aniseed
2 cups chicken stock
¼ cup cognac
½ cup Pernod
4 sprigs of cilantro, for garnish
1 medium lemon, sliced, for garnish

Brush the fish with the olive oil. Insert garlic into fish cavities. Sprinkle both sides of each fish with salt, pepper, thyme, and aniseed. Place the fish on a rack in a roasting pan. Combine the stock, cognac, and Pernod and pour into the pan under the fish. Cover tightly and bake at 475 degrees for 15 minutes. Remove lid and bake for 10 minutes more. Remove to serving plates, spoon liquid over fish, and garnish with lemon and cilantro.

 =Robert Mondavi Winery Coastal Chardonnay

MARY FRANN

MARY FRANN

Mary Frann is best known for her role as Bob Newhart's wife in the hit series "Newhart," which ran for eight years. She received praise for her role in "Fatal Charm" and the hit mini-series "Lucky Chances." Ms. Frann is involved in many charitable organizations, including the Starlight Foundation, which grants wishes to seriously ill children, the National Easter Seal Telethon, and the Amanda Foundation, which rescues abandoned animals.

Dear Paul—
All best for your book!

Mary Frann

Braised Venison with Fruit Compote

(Serves 4)

2 cups beef stock

1 large Granny Smith apple, peeled, cored, quartered, and diced

⅓ cup dried figs

⅓ cup dried apricots

⅓ cup dried prunes

2 tablespoons dried cranberries

2 tablespoons dried cherries

2 red chili peppers

1 cup chicken stock

2 tablespoons olive oil

8 venison medallions, trimmed of all fat and seasoned with black pepper

Chopped parsley, for garnish

Bring beef stock to a boil and reduce by half. Add apple, figs, apricots, prunes, cranberries, cherries, chili peppers, and chicken stock. Bring to a boil, cover, and simmer for 20 to 30 minutes. Heat the olive oil in a large skillet over medium heat and sauté the venison medallions for 3 to 5 minutes on each side, or until done. Place 2 medallions on each plate and ladle the fruit compote over the top. Garnish with parsley.

=*Robert Mondavi Winery Carneros District Pinot Noir*

VIC DAMONE

Vic Damone's name is woven in the American vocabulary as one of the most gifted and celebrated vocalists in history. He has recorded over two thousand songs, including such classics as "An Affair to Remember," "On the Street Where You Live," "Gigi," "Ebb Tide," "Why Was I Born" and "You're Breaking My Heart." Vic was recently awarded the President's Medal from Hofstra University and was also inducted into the Songwriter's Hall of Fame.

Linguine and Clams

(Serves 4)

Fresh rinsed clams
1 6 oz. jar of clam juice
8 plum tomatoes, chopped
4 tablespoons full-bodied olive oil
4 tablespoons cilantro
4 cloves of chopped garlic
1 teaspoon kosher salt
Fresh ground pepper
1 pound linguine

In separate pan add 2 tablespoons olive oil, heat. When oil is hot add clams. (Be sure clams are dry from rinsing. This will avoid any "splattering.") Cover, steam for 3–5 minutes until clams begin to open. Set to the side.

In separate large sauce pan add 2 tablespoons olive oil. Heat pan. When olive oil is hot add chopped garlic and cook until golden. Add chopped tomatoes. Cook until tomatoes begin to break down. Add salt and pepper and two pinches of cilantro. From cooked clams combine previously set aside juice to tomato mixture.

In separate pan boil linguine. When linguine is three quarters of the way cooked take off heat and drain. Combine linguine with tomato mixture. When the linguine is al denté, add clams to warm. Garnish dish with cilantro.

= Woodbridge Chardonnay

ALANA STEWART

With her down-to-earth, homegrown charm, Alana Stewart appeals to America's heartland. An actress as well as a top model and cover girl, she takes pride in her career and her role as a mom. She is a deeply spiritual woman, committed to the family, good health, and the planet. Her films include *Sgt. Pepper's Lonely Hearts Club Band*, *Swing Shift*, and *Where the Boys Are*.

Love,
Alana Stewart

Fettuccine in Pepper Cream Sauce

(Serves 4)

1 can chicken broth
2 tablespoons coarsely ground black pepper
½ cup cream
3 tablespoons flour
1 pound fettuccine, prepared according to package directions
Grated parmesan cheese, to taste

Combine the broth and pepper in a saucepan. Blend the cream and flour in a small bowl. Bring broth to a boil and whisk in the cream mixture, stirring constantly, to make a gravy. Remove from the heat and pour over the pasta. Add grated parmesan cheese.

 =*Woodbridge Chardonnay*

RITA RUDNER

RITA RUDNER

Rita Rudner's regular appearances in the late Eighties on "The Tonight Show," "Late Night with David Letterman," and "Comic Relief" established her as one of the country's premier stand-up comedians. She made her film debut in *Peter's Friends* alongside Emma Thompson and Kenneth Branagh. Her first book was published in 1993 and became a best-seller. The audio version received a Grammy nomination.

Spaghetti With Gummy Bears

(Serves 1)

Boil spaghetti. Drain. Add gummy bears. Mix. Eat. Call doctor.

Exploding Potato

(Serves 1)

Preheat oven to 550 degrees. Put many potatoes in oven. Do not puncture potatoes with fork before placing in oven. Forget about potatoes in oven till you hear a big bang. Run to oven and turn it off. Open oven. Scrape the bits of exploded potato off the oven. Eat. The potato is crunchy but you have used no oil. Buy new oven!

 =Mylanta

DONNA KARAN

Donna Karan trained at Parsons School of Design. She entered the fashion industry designing for Anne Klein and became head of the design team there. She left in 1984 and founded her own company in 1985 with the Essentials line, seven easy pieces every woman should have. Essentials became a success and was broadened to two hundred pieces. In 1988 the DKNY collection was introduced and has developed into the pillar of the Donna Karan label, which continues to include Essentials as well as Donna Karan cosmetics, Donna Karan Signature Gold Label, and Donna Karan Kids. She also has Donna Karan coffee blends and licenses for eyewear, socks, shoes, and patterns. Ms. Karan is interested in Eastern philosophy and meditation. She became a published author with her book *Modern Souls*.

Garlic Thyme Grilled Chicken

(Serves 8 to 10)

15 garlic cloves, chopped
Juice of 2 lemons
⅓ cup olive oil
1 teaspoon salt
1 teaspoon freshly ground black pepper
1 generous pinch of crushed red pepper
1 tablespoon dried thyme leaves
¼ cup dijon mustard
¼ cup white wine
2 kosher or free-range chickens, cut into 8 pieces each

Mix all the ingredients, except the chicken, into a marinade. Marinate the chicken in the mixture for 1 hour. Broil the chicken, bone side up, until golden. Turn the chicken and repeat. Remove chicken from the broiler and bake at 350 degrees for 12 minutes.

 =Woodbridge Chardonnay

ZSA ZSA GABOR

This is Zsa Zsa's love potion. This is what she cooks to catch a man and also what she cooks to keep one!

☆

Zsa Zsa Gabor made her stage debut at the age of fifteen in Vienna, Austria. This outgoing actress has acted in many films, including *Lovely to Look At* and *Every Girl Should Have One*. She is also an author, having written *How to Get a Man, How to Keep a Man, How to Get Rid of a Man*.

JOHN ENGSTEAD

Dracula Goulash

SZÉKELY GULYÁS

(Serves 6 to 8)

1 onion, diced
3 tablespoons butter
1 pound pork stew meat
1 pound veal stew meat
Paprika
Salt, to taste
1 tablespoon caraway seeds
4 pounds sauerkraut
2 pounds Hungarian or Polish sausage, cut into chunks
½ cup sour cream

Sauté onion in butter until yellow. Add pork and veal, enough paprika to make goulash red, salt, caraway seeds, and 2 cups of water and simmer for 2 hours. Rinse the sauerkraut and add to the meat. Add the sausage and cook for 30 minutes more. Add the sour cream on top just before serving.

 = *Robert Mondavi Winery Napa Valley Pinot Noir*

JOE DIFFIE

Some of my favorite memories are those of my mother and dad in the kitchen. They were ambassadors of sorts when it came to experimenting with new recipes and trying new foods, encouraging my two sisters and me to "try a bite" and "see if you like it." I feel this attitude served to broaden my perspective not only in the culinary world but also in everyday life as well. While on family trips, we loved to stop and experience different sites or points of interest along the way. This included stops at various and assorted eating places, such as restaurants and bistros. If I may wax philosophical: Food is analogous to life. Sights, smells, and textures all combine to lend character to our lives. Bon Appétit!

Chicken Spectacular

(Serves 6)

1 jar dried beef
6 boneless, skinless chicken breasts
6 slices of bacon
1 cup sour cream
1 can cream of mushroom soup

Layer the bottom of a 13 × 9-inch baking dish with dried beef. Roll each chicken breast up and wrap with a slice of bacon, using a toothpick to hold it together. Lay the breasts on top of the dried beef. In a separate bowl, mix together the sour cream and soup. Pour over the chicken and cover with foil. Bake at 275 degrees for 3 hours. Take off foil for the last 10 minutes, to brown the top.

Joe Diffie is the first country singer to receive a Number One hit with his first song, "Home." His albums have consistently struck gold and platinum. Mr. Diffie is a tireless fundraiser for numerous charities. One close to his heart is a program that benefits children with disabilities, First Steps/Duncanwood School. He is an avid golfer, woodworker, and NASCAR fan in his spare time. His passion for music cannot be denied.

 =Robert Mondavi Winery Coastal Pinot Noir

JAMES BROWN

James Brown, better known simply as JB, is co-host of Fox's "NFL Sunday." He is also host of "The World's Funniest Home Videos." JB is very involved in humanitarian causes both locally and nationally. These include the National Greater Washington Urban League, March of Dimes, Special Olympics, and Big Brothers of America.

James Brown

Crab Bake Imperial

(Serves 4 to 6)

4 tablespoons (½ stick) butter
3 tablespoons flour
1½ cups half-and-half
1 pound lump crabmeat, drained
2 teaspoons chopped parsley
1½ teaspoons dry mustard
½ teaspoon salt
2 teaspoons prepared horseradish
1 teaspoon wine Worcestershire sauce
1 cup bread crumbs
2 tablespoons butter, melted

Combine the 4 tablespoons butter, flour, and half-and-half in a large skillet and heat over low heat until smooth. Stir in the crabmeat, parsley, mustard, salt, horseradish, and wine Worcestershire, stirring gently. Spoon the mixture into a casserole dish. Combine the bread crumbs and the melted butter and sprinkle over the top of the crab mixture. Bake at 350 degrees for 30 minutes, or until bubbly.

= Robert Mondavi Winery Coastal Chardonnay

SHIRLEY JONES

Shirley Jones won an Academy Award for her portrayal of Lulu Baines in *Elmer Gantry*. She became the "Partridge Family" mom after movies like *Oklahoma!*, *The Music Man*, and *Carousel*. Other films include *The Cheyenne Social Club* and *The Family Nobody Wanted*. She is married to entertainer and talent agent Marty Ingels.

SHIRLEY JONES

Shirley's City Chicken

(Serves 8 to 10)

1 pound cubed beef
1 pound cubed pork
1 pound cubed veal
8 to 10 wooden skewers
2 eggs, lightly beaten
Cracker meal
Butter or margarine, for frying and dotting
Chopped herbs, to taste
Salt and pepper, to taste
Hot cooked rice or buttered noodles, for serving

Thread the meat on skewers, alternating a piece of beef, pork, and veal. Dip each entire skewer into eggs and cracker meal until completely coated. Melt butter in a large skillet over medium heat and brown skewers on all sides. Place in a casserole dish with herbs, salt, and pepper and dot with butter. Cover and bake at 300 degrees for about 1 hour 45 minutes, basting a few times. Uncover and bake about 30 minutes more. Serve with rice or buttered noodles.

= Robert Mondavi Winery Pinot Noir

MITCH GAYLORD

BARRY KING

Mitch Gaylord, who won gold and silver medals in the 1984 Olympics, is an outstanding gymnast admired by millions of people around the world for his athletic abilities. He is writing a book that focuses on training the body and the mind for inner fulfillment in all endeavors of life. He has appeared in the movies *American Tiger* and *Animal Instincts*.

Spicy Tuna Pasta

(Serves 4)

2 tablespoons olive oil
1 garlic clove, chopped
8 plum tomatoes, seeded and cubed
¼ cup chopped basil
1 tablespoon Dijon mustard
1 teaspoon salt
1 teaspoon black pepper
Crushed red pepper
1 teaspoon oregano
½ cup white wine
1 can (8 ounces) V8 juice
1 can tuna, (12 ounces) drained
1 pound penne or linguine, cooked

Heat the olive oil in a sauté pan and cook the garlic. Add the tomatoes and basil and cook over medium heat for 10 minutes. Add the mustard, salt, black pepper, red pepper, and oregano. Cook for 5 minutes more on high heat, then add the wine and V8 and simmer for 5 minutes more. Just before serving, add the tuna and heat it through. Serve with hot pasta.

 = Robert Mondavi Winery Coastal Chardonnay

JOSÉ EBER

When I was a boy growing up in Nice, France, my mother used to make the most fabulous Boeuf Bourguignon. It is a wonderful recipe that has been handed down in my family for many generations. I hope that this little taste of France finds its way into your home too!

☆

José Eber has been described as intense yet gentle. Women who normally keep tight control over every aspect of their lives flock to him and relinquish control of their hair to his superior skill and talent. He is not a world-renowned French hair stylist, but rather *the* world-renowned French hairstylist. He created the tousled look for Farrah Fawcett that to this day remains the most copied hairstyle in the world. He also counts Elizabeth Taylor and Cher among his clients. He is currently building an empire that includes a chain of high-style salons, book deals, videos, and a hair care line. If history is any judge, José Eber will be wildly successful at creating an empire with class and elegance.

JOSÉ EBER

Beef Bourguignon

(Serves 6)

8 ounces mushrooms, sliced
4 tablespoons (½ stick) margarine or butter
3 slices of bacon, cooked and cut into small pieces
2 pounds beef tenderloin or sirloin steak, cut into cubes
2 tablespoons flour
2 garlic cloves, crushed
1 tablespoon tomato paste
1 cup red wine
2 beef bouillon cubes, dissolved in 2 cups hot water
2 tablespoons sugar
¼ teaspoon salt
¼ teaspoon dried thyme leaves
1 small bay leaf

For serving: hot cooked rice, salad, garlic bread

Sauté the mushrooms in butter, remove, and set aside. Add the bacon to the mushrooms. Add the beef to the pan and brown. As it browns, blend in the flour, garlic, tomato paste, wine, dissolved bouillon cubes, sugar, salt, thyme, and bay leaf. Mix the mushrooms and bacon with the beef mixture. Place in a casserole dish and bake at 350 degrees for 3 hours. Serve with rice, salad, and garlic bread.

=Robert Mondavi Winery Cabernet Sauvignon

TRACY LAWRENCE

Tracy Lawrence

In less than five years Tracy Lawrence has earned a permanent place in the hearts of country fans. He has sold over five million albums, had eleven chart-topping hits, and won several awards. Tracy performs for many benefits and charitable organizations to raise funds for AIDS research, a homeless shelter for women and children, flood and hurricane disaster relief, and the American Cancer Society.

B-B-Q Meatballs

(Serves 6)

1 pound ground round
1 small onion, finely chopped
1 teaspoon oregano
¼ teaspoon pepper
B-B-Que Sauce (recipe follows) or bottled sauce

Mix the meat, onion, oregano, and pepper and shape into about 30 meatballs. Place on a baking sheet. Bake at 450 degrees for about 20 minutes, or until brown and done. Place the meatballs in a deep dish and pour the sauce on top. Serve hot.

B-B-Q Sauce

(Makes about 4 cups)

1 cup cider vinegar
1 cup (packed) brown sugar
1 cup tomato sauce
1 can Coca-Cola
Juice of 1 lemon
Juice of 1 orange
8 tablespoons (1 stick) margarine
1½ teaspoons cayenne (optional)

Combine all the ingredients including cayenne, if using, in a small saucepan and cook over low heat for about 20 minutes.

 = Woodbridge White Zinfandel

PATTI LABELLE

Patti LaBelle began her career in a Baptist choir. Her five-octave range has ensured phenomenal success for more than three decades. Music has sustained her through good times and bad, when she helplessly watched three of her sisters die of cancer. A Grammy winner, she has won admiration not only for her music but for her extensive charity work.

GEORGE HOLZ

Love, Patti LaBelle

Barbecued Shrimp for Two

24 large shrimp

Seasoning Mix

1 teaspoon cayenne
1 teaspoon black pepper
½ teaspoon crushed red pepper
½ teaspoon salt
½ teaspoon dried thyme leaves
½ teaspoon dried rosemary leaves, crushed
⅛ teaspoon dried oregano
12 tablespoons (1½ sticks) unsalted butter
1½ teaspoons minced garlic
1½ teaspoons Worcestershire sauce
½ cup fish stock
¼ cup beer, at room temperature
French bread or hot cooked rice, for serving

Peel and devein the shrimps, then rinse in cold water and drain. Set aside.

In a small bowl combine the 7 seasoning mix ingredients. Combine 1 stick of the butter, the garlic, Worcestershire, and seasoning mix in a large skillet over high heat. When the butter is melted, add the shrimp. Cook for about 2 minutes, shaking the pan gently back and forth. Add the remaining butter and fish stock and continue cooking and shaking for 2 to 3 minutes more. Add the beer and cook for 1 or 2 minutes. Remove from the heat. Serve immediately in bowls with lots of French bread for dipping or with rice.

= Robert Mondavi Winery Napa Valley Zinfandel

TRAVIS TRITT

Travis Tritt's successful writing style combines classic country with the exciting mix of rock and rhythm and blues. This style has come to be known as Southern rock—one example is Tritt's huge hit, "Here's a Quarter (Call Someone Who Cares)." In his book *Ten Feet Tall and Bulletproof*, he stated that his induction into country music's historic Grand Ole Opry was one of the greatest things that ever happened to him.

Hot and Spicy Chili

(Serves 6 to 8)

1 pound ground beef
2 cans (15 ounces) New Orleans–style kidney beans, drained
2 cans (14 ½ ounces each) stewed tomatoes
1 small can (6 ounces) tomato paste
1 can (12 ounces) beer
1 large bell pepper, coarsely chopped
1 medium onion, coarsely chopped
2 tablespoons hot chili powder
½ teaspoon minced garlic
3 tablespoons yellow mustard
2 tablespoons chopped basil
½ teaspoon oregano
2 jalapenos, sliced
Hot'n Spicy seasoned salt, to taste
Your favorite cheese, shredded
Tabasco sauce, to taste

Brown the ground beef, drain, and transfer to a crock pot. Add the remaining ingredients, except the cheese and Tabasco, and mix well. Cook on low for 8 to 10 hours or on high for 3 to 4 hours. Cover with your favorite shredded cheese, add Tabasco, and enjoy!

Tip: **Have plenty of Pepto-Bismol on hand.**

 =Woodbridge Zinfandel

MELBA MOORE

TONY METAXAS

If you can't sing, after eating this chicken you will!

☆

Melba Moore is a Tony Award winner and two-time Grammy nominee. Her talent has earned her a rewarding career in recording, theater, television, music, and film. In addition, she has designed a signature line of products for those who work out of the home. A percentage of sales from these products and her other endeavors helps support the Melba Moore Foundation for Children, a nonprofit organization that funds various charities for needy youth. Ms. Moore has seen both the up and down sides of life, and she knows what it means to get a helping hand when you really need it.

Melba Moore

Melba Moore's Zingin' Singin' Chicken

(Serves 4 to 6)

1 lemon
1 tablespoon seasoned salt
1 sprig of rosemary or 2 teaspoons dried rosemary leaves, crushed
Pepper, to taste
Granulated garlic or garlic powder, to taste
1 fryer chicken (about 3½ pounds)
¼ cup vermouth (optional)
1 Bermuda onion, quartered
Steamed or lightly sautéed vegetables and sliced tomatoes, for serving

This is the most important key to the recipe: Pierce the lemon repeatedly with a fork in as many areas as possible. Mix the seasoned salt, rosemary, pepper, and granulated garlic in a bowl. Wash the chicken inside and out and pat dry. Sprinkle vermouth, if using, inside the cavity and on the outside. Then sprinkle the seasoning mixture inside the cavity and on the outside. Insert 2 quarters of the onion, the lemon, and the remaining 2 quarters of the onion in the cavity of the bird.

Cover with foil and bake on a roasting rack in a shallow pan at 350 degrees for three 30-minute intervals. After each interval turn the chicken over. Piercing the lemon and turning the chicken allow the lemon juice to permeate the chicken. The meat is succulent and wonderful. Garnish with cooked vegetables and sliced tomatoes for a fabulous meal.

=*Robert Mondavi Winery Coastal Chardonnay*

CONNIE STEVENS

Food not only sustains the life of the body but the life of the soul. It's comfort and memories and cause for celebration. Cooking for someone is a loving, selfless act. We should always keep that in mind and appreciate the cook.

CONNIE STEVENS

Connie Stevens has earned an international reputation in show business with her career on the Broadway stage, in motion pictures, television, recordings, and concerts. Among her movie credits are *Back to the Beach, Tapeheads,* and *Palm Springs Weekend.* She has recently experienced success with her beauty line "Forever Spring: The Beauty System." Ms. Stevens devotes much of her time to such philanthropic endeavors as a Native American youth organization called Windfeather, and Dignity, which helps the mentally and physically handicapped become working members of the community. With a hectic working schedule of film and television commitments, writing, producing, and personal appearances, Connie Stevens is a true superstar.

Bolognese Sauce

(Serves 8)

4 tablespoons olive oil

1 tablespoon butter

1 large onion, finely chopped

1 large garlic clove, minced

1 medium carrot, finely chopped

2 large cans tomato purée

2 tablespoons tomato paste

1 large can of plum tomatoes, passed through a sieve, pulp discarded

4 ounces ground pork

4 ounces ground veal

4 ounces ground beef

Salt and pepper, to taste

½ teaspoon sugar

¼ cup minced Italian flat-leaf parsley

¼ cup minced basil

¼ cup cream

2 pounds pasta, cooked

Grated parmesan cheese, to taste

Heat 2 tablespoons of the olive oil and the butter in a large pot and sauté the onion, garlic, and carrot until the onion is translucent. Add the tomato purée, tomato paste, and the puréed canned tomatoes and simmer.

Heat the remaining 2 tablespoons of olive oil in another pan and sauté the ground meats until the meat is no longer pink. Using a slotted spoon, transfer the meat to the simmering tomato mixture. Add salt, pepper, and sugar. Simmer for 1 hour. Add the parsley and basil. Simmer for 30 minutes more. Add the cream and turn off the heat. Serve over cooked pasta. Top with grated parmesan cheese.

=*Robert Mondavi Winery Pinot Noir*

SALLY KIRKLAND

SALLY KIRKLAND

Sally Kirkland is best known for her performance in *Anna*, which won her an Academy Award nomination and the Golden Globe and Independent Spirit awards. Her other starring roles include *Revenge, Cold Feet, Best of the Best, JFK,* and *Cheatin' Hearts*. She is a producer, theater and TV director, acting teacher, yoga master, and ordained minister. Look for her in the upcoming movie *Ed TV* co-starring Matthew McConaughey and Woody Harrelson.

love And light

Sally Kirkland

Sally's Tiger Shrimp in Mustard Sauce

(Serves 4)

¼ each *red, green, and yellow bell peppers, cut into strips*
½ *medium onion, thinly sliced and separated into rings*
1 tablespoon olive oil
Salt and pepper, to taste; 2 garlic cloves, mashed
1 tablespoon condensed chicken broth or 1 can (15 ounces) chicken broth
White wine; Juice of 1 small lemon
1 heaping tablespoon Dijon mustard
1 tablespoon chopped parsley; Dash of mace
1 pound tiger shrimp in the shell, butterflied and deveined

Hot cooked rice or pasta, for serving
Sprigs of parsley, for garnish
Lemon wedges, for garnish

Cook the pepper strips and onion rings in olive oil in a frying pan over very high heat with salt, pepper, and garlic, stirring constantly, until the onions are slightly browned and the peppers are cooked but still firm. If using condensed broth, mix 1 cup hot water and 1 cup wine and add the broth. If using canned broth, mix with white wine to make 2 cups. Add the lemon juice, mustard, parsley, and mace and blend thoroughly. Add this liquid to the onion-pepper mixture. Place on low heat and simmer gently for 8 to 10 minutes, or until it is all mixed together.

Bring the sauce to a hard boil and plunge the shrimp into it, stirring constantly for 3 to 5 minutes, or until the shrimp turn red. Do not leave them in the sauce for too long, or they will get tough. Serve over any kind of rice or pasta, using as much of the sauce as you like. Decorate with sprigs of parsley and wedges of lemon.

 = *Robert Mondavi Winery Chardonnay*

KIM FIELDS FREEMAN

Kim Fields Freeman

Kim Fields Freeman first appeared as Tootie in the television series "The Facts of Life," which ran for nine successful years. Then she went on to earn her degree from Pepperdine University. She returned to acting as Regine Hunter in the television series "Living Single."

Great French Fries

(Serves 1)

1 cup get-in-car
2 tablespoons drive-to-McDonalds
½ gallon order-your-fries
2 teaspoons eat-'em-and-lick-yo'-fingers!

All good cooks should always label containers they place in the refrigerator. Or else something might happen like what happened to me when I was young. One day I came running into the apartment from playing outside. I busted into the kitchen and headed to the fridge, pulled the door open, and grabbed one of those glass Tropicana Orange Juice bottles that people always reuse for water, iced tea, etc. Thinking I was about to quench my thirst with tea, I ended up chugging down some fish grease!!

=*Milk Shake*

JACKLYN ZEMAN

JACKLYN ZEMAN

Jacklyn Zeman does it all—
wife, mother, actress, author.
She has played the popular
role of Bobbie Spencer on
ABC's "General Hospital" for
nearly twenty years and has
appeared in more than three
thousand episodes. This
likable actress is a true
contemporary role model.
Travel is a favorite pastime
and it has been incorporated
into her appearances on
"Lifestyles of the Rich and
Famous." She strongly
believes that education is the
key to achieving one's goals.

Jacklyn Zeman

Gazpacho Pasta

(Serves 4)

6 ounces spaghetti
Vegetable oil cooking spray
1 cup broccoli florets
1 cup thinly sliced carrots
1 cup sliced zucchini
¼ cup sliced onion
1 small yellow bell pepper, cut into julienne strips
¼ cup sliced cucumber
½ cup sliced mushrooms
1 small tomato, cut into 8 wedges
2 tablespoons dry vermouth
6 tablespoons grated parmesan cheese
1 tablespoon minced parsley
¼ teaspoon crushed red pepper

Cook pasta according to package directions, omitting salt and fat. Drain and set aside. Coat a large nonstick skillet with cooking spray. Place over medium heat until hot. Add the broccoli, carrots, zucchini, and onion and sauté for 4 minutes. Add the pepper strips, cucumber, and mushrooms and sauté for 4 minutes more. Add the pasta, tomato, and vermouth and toss gently. Cook until thoroughly heated. Sprinkle with cheese, parsley, and red pepper and toss gently. Serve immediately.

 = *Woodbridge Sauvignon Blanc*

GLORIA GAYNOR

Gloria Gaynor, officially crowned Queen of Disco in the Big Apple, earned the title First Lady of Disco for her popularity and her many firsts in the disco era. She was the first—and only—artist to receive a Grammy for Best Disco Recording. Gloria's recording of "I Will Survive" is as popular today as the day she first sang it. Other well-known hits are "Never Can Say Goodbye," "Most of All," and "Anybody Wanna Party." In addition to recording, she continues to tour worldwide, appear at book signings, and model for designer fashions. She is working on a film project based on her book *I Will Survive*.

Chicken à la Gaynor

(Serves 4)

1 fryer chicken (about 3½ pounds) cut up
Seasoned salt or salt and pepper, to taste
1 cup cream of chicken soup
2 tablespoons cooking sherry
1 cup sour cream
½ cup milk
1 can (13 ounces) sliced mushrooms
1 teaspoon dried tarragon
Hot cooked saffron rice, for serving
Vegetables, for serving

Lightly season chicken with seasoned salt or salt and pepper. Place in a shallow baking dish and bake at 425 degrees for 40 minutes, or until golden brown and crispy on top.

While the chicken bakes, prepare sauce on top of the stove in a saucepan. Mix the soup and sherry over low heat until smooth. Slowly add the sour cream, stirring constantly to keep the mixture smooth. Add milk, mushrooms, and tarragon. When chicken is done, pour this mixture over it and put back in the oven for 15 minutes. Serve with saffron rice and colorful vegetables for an attractive, delicious, and quick meal that tastes as if you've been cooking this gourmet's delight for hours.

=Robert Mondavi Winery Napa Valley Pinot Noir

SHARON GLESS

Sharon Gless is best known for her seven-year run playing Detective Chris Cagney on the highly acclaimed TV series "Cagney & Lacey" with Tyne Daly. She has also appeared in numerous films. Sharon has won two Golden Globes and four Q awards. She also appeared in "Marcus Welby, M.D." from 1974 to 1976 with Robert Young.

SHARON GLESS

Believe in your dreams!

Sharon Gless

Reza's Tandoori Chicken

(Serves 8)

5 pounds chicken legs, thighs, and breasts
Juice of 2 lemons
1 tablespoon kosher salt
½ cup plain yogurt
1 medium onion, coarsely chopped
1 clove garlic, coarsely chopped
1 piece fresh ginger about 1½ inches square
½ to 1 hot green chili, sliced
1 tablespoon garam masala

Skin the chicken pieces. Cut each breast into 4 pieces. Detach legs from thighs if necessary. Cut deep diagonal slits in all the chicken pieces, slitting the legs on 2 sides, the breasts and thighs only on the meaty side. Place the chicken on a baking sheet and sprinkle with the lemon juice and salt. Rub the lemon juice and salt into each piece of chicken. Let stand for 15 to 20 minutes.

Purée the remaining ingredients in a blender or food processor. Spoon or brush this mixture on the chicken, making sure it gets into all the slits. Place the chicken in a large stainless steel, glass, or ceramic bowl. Cover with plastic and refrigerate for at least 12 to 18 hours.

Arrange the chicken on a baking sheet and preheat the broiler. Broil for 15 to 20 minutes, turning once, or until the chicken is cooked through but not browned. Breasts may be done as soon as 10 minutes.

Tip: Garam masala is available in specialty food stores.

= Robert Mondavi Winery Coastal Chardonnay

JOANNA KERNS

Joanna Kerns is famous for her starring role as Maggie Sever in "Growing Pains" with Alan Thicke. Before that she was a gymnast and competed in Olympic trials. Her film credits include *Sisters and Other Strangers*, Robin Cook's *Mortal Fear*, and *Mother Knows Best*.

JOANNA KERNS

Joanna's Pasta with Broccoli and Leeks

(Serves 4 to 6)

¼ cup olive oil
8 to 10 garlic cloves, sliced
4 leeks, well washed and sliced
salt, to taste
1 bunch of broccoli, florets separated
1 pound pasta, such as fettucine, spaghetti, penne, or rigatoni, cooked

Heat the olive oil and brown the garlic. Add the leeks and slowly cook, stirring regularly, until almost caramelized. Add salt. Add the broccoli and cook for about 5 minutes. Add the pasta to the leeks and broccoli. Toss and serve. (Leftovers can be refrigerated.)

=Robert Mondavi Winery Coastal Chardonnay

JO MARIE PAYTON

I love food, I love people, I love myself—which is why I would not give anyone anything to eat I wouldn't eat myself!

☆

Jo Marie Payton is best known as the effervescent mom, Harriette Winslow, of "Family Matters," which ran for nine seasons. Her character actually began two years earlier in the TV series "Perfect Strangers." She was such a hit the producers created "Family Matters" as a spin-off series to star her with Reginald Vel-Johnson. She is deeply committed to education and has created the Frankie Payton Scholarship Fund at the State University of New York at Albany in honor of her mother. She also hosts the Jo Marie Payton Celebrity Classic, which raises scholarship funds for the university.

One-pot Poultry Passion

(Serves 6)

¼ cup oil, butter, or margarine
2 pounds chicken or turkey parts
1 cup chopped onion
½ cup chopped bell pepper
2 tablespoons Worcestershire sauce
1 garlic clove, crushed
½ teaspoon dried thyme leaves
½ teaspoon paprika
½ teaspoon celery salt
Salt and pepper, to taste
2 cups rice, rinsed and drained
1 cup frozen peas or mixed vegetables
¼ cup tomato paste

Heat the oil in a large skillet or saucepan on medium-high heat. Add the chicken or turkey pieces and brown, about 5 minutes. Add the onion, bell pepper, Worcestershire, garlic, thyme, paprika, celery salt, salt, and pepper. Cook for about 5 minutes, being careful not to burn the mixture. Add 3 cups of water and bring to a boil. Add the rice, peas, and tomato paste. Cook on high heat for 20 to 30 minutes, depending on the texture of rice you prefer. Let stand for 7 minutes, then serve.

=*Robert Mondavi Winery Napa Valley Chardonnay*

MAJEL BARRETT RODDENBERRY

Majel Barrett Roddenberry played Nurse Christine Chapel in the original "Star Trek." She played Lwaxana Troi in "Star Trek: The Next Generation" and "Star Trek: Deep Space Nine" and plays Lady Morella in "Babylon 5." Both "Star Trek: The Next Generation" and "Babylon 5," along with "Star Trek: Voyager" and the *Star Trek* films, feature her unique voice as the Federation computer. Her latest character is Dr. Julianne Belman in the TV series "Gene Roddenberry's Earth: Final Conflict." Mrs. Roddenberry carries on the legacy of her late husband, Gene Roddenberry, as executive producer.

MAJEL BARRETT RODDENBERRY

Kumquat Chicken

(Serves 40)

2 pounds cashew nuts
4 teaspoons ground nutmeg
40 boneless, skinless chicken breasts
4 eggs, beaten with 2 teaspoons water
1 pound (4 sticks) butter
14 green scallions, chopped
10 sprigs of parsley, chopped
Paprika, for sprinkling
Sweet-and-Sour Kumquat Sauce (recipe follows)
4 cups all-purpose flour, seasoned with salt and pepper

Grind the cashews in a food processor until fine. Mix with the nutmeg. Dip the chicken breasts in egg then roll them in the ground cashew mix. Place on foil-lined baking sheets. Dot the breasts with butter and sprinkle with scallions, parsley, and paprika. (Can be frozen at this point for up to 2 weeks).

Place chicken on middle rack of oven and bake at 350 degrees for 15 to 20 minutes, or just until done. Do not overbake. Serve with the kumquat sauce.

Sweet-and-Sour Kumquat Sauce

(Makes about 2 quarts)

½ pound (2 sticks) butter
1 cup slivered blanched almonds
4 cans (13½ ounces each) pineapple tidbits, drained
⅔ cup (packed) brown sugar
1 cup white vinegar
2 cups pineapple juice

2 cups preserved kumquats
⅓ cup cornstarch

*M*elt the butter in a saucepan. Add the almonds and pineapple tidbits and stir over medium-low heat until lightly browned. Stir in the brown sugar until smooth and bubbling. Add the vinegar, pineapple juice, and kumquats. Stir well. Mix cornstarch with ¼ cup cold water until smooth. Stir into the sauce until smooth and thickened. (Can be prepared several days ahead of time and reheated.)

 =*La Famiglia Tocai Friulano*

STEFANIE POWERS

Cooking is a very personal thing to all of us. Generally, our palate is shaped by the way we are raised. So I often think of my grandmother, who gave this recipe to my mother, so that I can give it to you.

Pierogie

(Serves 8 to 10)

Dough

2½ pounds all-purpose flour
4 eggs
2 cups sour cream
Salt, to taste
Warm water

Mix together the flour, eggs, sour cream, and salt and add just enough water to make a dough. Knead in the bowl, cover with a towel, and let stand for 10 minutes. Cut off a piece, place on a floured board, and roll out. Cut into squares, fill with the cheese or sauerkraut filling, and pinch together.

Cheese Filling

2 big potatoes, peeled and cooked
¼ pound (1 stick) margarine
Salt and pepper, to taste
2 pounds pot cheese or hoop cheese
3 eggs

Mash the potatoes with the margarine. Add the other ingredients and mix together well.

Sauerkraut Filling

1 can (1 pound) sauerkraut
1 medium onion, sliced
¼ pound (1 stick) margarine
Salt and pepper, to taste

Rinse off the sauerkraut juice, add water, and pour off. Add water to cover and cook for 20 minutes. Rinse and squeeze dry. Fry the onion in the margarine, add to the sauerkraut, and mix. Add salt and pepper. Mix well. Ready to be added to dough.

Cook the pierogie in salted water. When they float on top, they are done.

Stefanie Powers is an attractive, athletic brunette, and a leading lady of Hollywood pictures, but she is most recognized as Jennifer Hart from the immensely successful television series "Hart to Hart." Some of her other starring roles have been the TV miniseries "Mistral's Daughter" and "Hollywood Wives" as well as "Hart to Hart Returns." Some of her films include *Experiment in Terror* and *McLintock!* In addition to her acting, she has her own production company and is president of the William Holden Wildlife Foundation, dedicated to the preservation of wild animals in Kenya. The foundation demands a lot of travel, but when she is at home she enjoys her pets and takes care of her horses.

=Robert Mondavi Winery Napa Valley Pinot Noir

HUGH HEFNER

Hugh Hefner, founder and editor-in-chief of Playboy, has influenced society with the world's best-selling men's magazine. He started his magazine on his kitchen table in a South Side Chicago apartment in 1953 with $8,000. The cover of the first issue in December was a calendar photo of Marilyn Monroe. It sold more than seventy thousand copies—enough to finance another issue! In 1971, when Playboy Enterprises went public, the magazine was selling more than seven million copies a month. They also had twenty-three Playboy clubs, a TV and motion picture company, a record label, a book publishing company, and a modeling agency. Mr. Hefner had created an empire! He is currently working on his long-awaited autobiography.

Hugh Hefner

PLAYBOY ENTERPRISES, INC.

Pot Roast Dinner

(Serves 4)

1 blade-cut chuck roast (4 to 7 pounds)
1 tablespoon seasoning salt
1 teaspoon ground white pepper
1 tablespoon garlic salt
2 cups all-purpose flour
1 cup vegetable oil
½ pound (2 sticks) lightly salted butter
1½ cups coarsely chopped onion
1 cup coarsely chopped carrot
1 cup coarsely chopped celery
¼ cup Gravy Master
4 small red potatoes, peeled
Sea salt and ground white pepper, to taste
Cooked corn on the cob, whole kernel corn, cream-style corn, or peas, for serving (optional)

Trim all the excess fat off the roast. Season with seasoning salt, white pepper, and garlic salt on both sides. Coat heavily with flour, reserving the remaining flour for roux. Pour the vegetable oil in the bottom of a heavy roasting pan and heat over medium heat. Place the roast in the pan and brown well on each side. Remove from the pan and pour off the fat. Scrape up and set aside the brown bits stuck to the bottom of the pan.

Melt the butter in the pan and add the reserved flour to make a roux. Cook until the roux is a rich brown color. Add enough water to make a generous amount of gravy. The consistency should be thin at this point. Add the onion, carrot, celery, and Gravy Master. Add the pot roast and drippings. Cover and bake at 350 degrees for 4 hours.

Boil the potatoes in salted water until tender. Drain, cover with foil, and keep warm. When ready to serve, thin the pot roast gravy with water if too thick and adjust for taste with salt and pepper. If too thin, cook down to a medium consistency. Strain the gravy into a serving bowl. Cut

2 chunks of meat for each person, place on a plate with gravy, and serve with the potatoes and vegetables. If desired, serve also with corn on the cob, whole kernel corn, cream-style corn, or peas.

Tip: Order a blade-cut chuck roast from the butcher, the *second* cut from the bottom of the blade, 2½ inches thick.

= *Robert Mondavi Coastal Cabernet Sauvignon*

BUDDY HACKETT

Many years ago, my father was given a monkey and a parrot as collateral for a sofa. In order to save money he ordered sunflower seeds and bananas in bulk. The family ate just seeds and bananas for five weeks! I have never had a potassium deficiency since, and that was sixty-two years ago!

Buddy Hackett is one of the funniest and most inventive American stand-up comics. His films include *Walking My Baby Back Home* and *The Love Bug*.

BUDDY HACKETT

Sweet-and-Sour Baked Fish

(Serves 4)

1 whole carp (2 to 3 pounds)
1 slice (⅛ in thick) fresh ginger
1 garlic clove
1 tablespoon peanut, corn, or other oil
About 2 tablespoons cornstarch, for coating fish
5 tablespoons sugar or Sweet'n Low
1 tablespoon lemon juice
3 tablespoons rice vinegar or red wine vinegar
2 tablespoons catsup
1 tablespoon soy sauce
1 tablespoon cornstarch dissolved in ½ cup cold water
About ⅓ cup oil, for frying

To prepare the fish for cooking, wash the fish inside and out, then pat it dry with paper towels. Rub the fish inside and out with the ginger and garlic. Rub the fish on the outside with the peanut oil, which will help keep the fish from sticking when it is cooked. Pat the 2 tablespoons cornstarch all over the outside of the fish. Set aside.

To prepare the sauce, combine the sugar, lemon juice, vinegar, catsup, and soy sauce in a 1-quart saucepan and bring to a boil. Reduce the heat and simmer, uncovered, for 2 to 3 minutes. Stir the cornstarch-water mixture until smooth. Blend the mixture into the sauce, stirring until it boils and thickens. Keep the sauce warm over very low heat.

To cook the fish, heat the oil in a wok or 12-inch skillet to 350 degrees. If the oil is too hot, the fish will stick. If you are using a wok, swish the oil around the sides so that the fish won't stick to the sides. Carefully place the fish in the pan or wok, and cook for 3 minutes, all the while spooning oil over the top of the fish. Cover the pan or wok and cook the fish for 5 to 10 minutes, depending on its size. Uncover and with 2 large spoons, carefully turn the fish over. Brown the other side for about 2 minutes. Very carefully transfer the fish to a large platter. Pour the sauce over the fish and serve immediately.

Tip: Choose a fish that fits comfortably in the pan or wok. Sea bass, red snapper, or cod may be substituted for carp.

 = *Woodbridge Merlot*

NINA BLACKWOOD

Over the years I have collected many cookbooks from the British Isles. Although not generally considered to be one of the world's great cuisines, British, Irish, and Scottish cookery is living history. Unfortunately, in the recent past, British cuisine has suffered a poor reputation. This decline was primarily due to the advent of tinned condiments and foodstuffs along with the forced rationing brought about by World Wars I and II. One need not dig too deeply, however, to find culinary treasures such as Stew of Dublin Bay Prawns and Asparagus in Saffron Soup, Salmon in Pastry with Herb Sauce, or Heather Honey and Whiskey Ice Cream. Mighty delectable fare, I'd say. British cuisine at its finest is a celebration of land and sea in its purest form. I love it for its honest earthiness.

☆

Nina Blackwood's first love is music. In 1978 she began experimenting in the field of music videos and by 1981 she became the first MTV V.J. For five years she was the on-camera host, interviewer, and music newscaster. That led to contracts with "Entertainment Tonight" as a music reporter and her own show, "The Rock Report." She was also co-host of the award-winning show "Solid Gold." Ms. Blackwood is committed to such charitable causes as world hunger and animal rights.

NINA BLACKWOOD

Salmon in Pastry with Herb Sauce

(Serves 6)

2 thick salmon fillets (about 2½ pounds), skinned and boned
Salt and pepper, to taste
6 tablespoons (¾ stick) butter
2 pieces ginger in syrup
1 generous tablespoon dried currants
Shortcrust Pastry (recipe follows)

Herb Sauce

4 tablespoons (½ stick) butter
2 shallots, chopped
1 tablespoon chopped parsley
2 teaspoons chopped chervil
2 teaspoons chopped tarragon
1 heaping teaspoon flour
1 cup cream
Salt and pepper
1 teaspoon dijon mustard
2 egg yolks
Lemon juice, to taste
1 egg, beaten, for glaze
Green salad, for serving

Season the fillets with salt and pepper. Mash the butter, chop the ginger, and mash it into the butter. Add currants to the mixture and place two thirds of it between the fillets. Spread the remaining mixture on top of the salmon.

Roll out the pastry ½ inch thick. Place the salmon on it and seal the edges of the pastry firmly around the fish. Cut away the excess pastry and carefully turn the salmon package over onto a greased baking sheet so that the seam is on the bottom. Slash the top of the pastry case in 3 places to allow steam to escape. If desired, make decorative little shapes out of the extra pastry and affix them on top with beaten egg. Brush the top with more beaten egg. Bake at 425 degrees for 30 minutes, or until golden brown.

To prepare the sauce, melt the butter in a pan, add the shallots, parsley, chervil, and tarragon, and cook over low heat until soft. Stir in the flour, all but 1 tablespoon of the cream, and season with salt and pepper. Simmer, stirring constantly, for 10 minutes, then blend in the mustard. Stir the egg yolks into the sauce. Continue to stir until it thickens slightly but do not let it boil. Correct the seasoning and add lemon juice. Serve the sauce separately. Goes great with a crisp salad, a dry Chardonnay, and good company!

Shortcrust Pastry

(Makes enough for a 2-crust pie)

1¼ cups all-purpose flour
½ teaspoon salt
4 tablespoons shortening
4 tablespoons (½ stick) butter or margarine
2 tablespoons cold water

This recipe is made with 4 parts flour to 2 parts fat, by weight. It has a crisp yet melt-in-the-mouth texture. This is achieved by rubbing the fat and flour together with your fingers to make a crumblike mixture with an even distribution of fat-coated flour. Sift the flour and salt into a bowl. Cut the shortening and butter into ½-inch cubes and distribute evenly over the flour. Rub lightly into the flour with your fingertips, lifting up the mixture to keep it as cool and airy as possible. Continue rubbing until the mixture resembles fine bread crumbs. Make a well in the center and add the cold water to produce a soft but not sticky dough. Turn the dough out onto a floured surface and roll it out.

= *Robert Mondavi Winery Coastal Chardonnay*

CLINT EASTWOOD

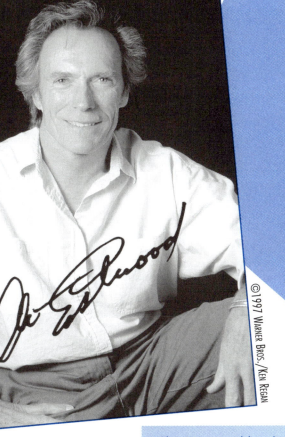

©1997 WARNER BROS./KEN REGAN

Clint Eastwood has been an actor, producer, director, mayor—you name it. He's won Best Picture and Best Director Oscars for *Unforgiven*. At age sixty-five he was given the honorary Irving Thalberg Award by the Academy. He recently produced, directed, and starred in the political thriller *Absolute Power*.

Spaghetti Western

(Serves 4)

3 tablespoons vegetable oil
½ cup chopped shallots
½ cup chopped celery
2 large garlic cloves, crushed
½ cup chopped red bell pepper
½ cup chopped yellow or green bell pepper
1 can (16 ounces) whole tomatoes
½ cup tomato purée
½ cup fish stock or bottled clam juice
1 bay leaf
1 teaspoon anchovy paste
½ teaspoon saffron threads or ground turmeric
Salt and freshly ground pepper, to taste
12 large mussels in the shell, scrubbed and debearded
1 package (10 ounces) frozen artichoke hearts, thawed and drained
4 jumbo shrimps, peeled and deveined
4 large sea scallops (about 4 ounces), quartered
½ cup heavy cream
2 tablespoons Pernod (optional)
1 can (6½ ounces) clams, drained and chopped
8 ounces spaghetti, cooked
Celery leaves, for garnish (optional)

Heat the oil in a deep 12-inch pan over medium heat. Add the shallots, celery, garlic, red and yellow peppers and cook, stirring frequently, for about 10 minutes, or until tender. Add the tomatoes with their liquid, tomato purée, fish stock, bay leaf, anchovy paste, saffron, salt, and pepper and bring to a boil. Reduce the heat to medium-low and simmer, covered, for 10 minutes.

Meanwhile, in a 3-quart saucepan, bring 1 inch of water to a boil. Add the mussels in the shell and cook, covered, just until the shells open, about 4 minutes. Drain. Using a sharp knife, cut the mussels away from shells. Reserve 12 half shells, discarding the rest. Rinse the mussels under cold water and set aside.

Add the artichoke hearts, shrimps, and scallops to the tomato sauce. Increase the heat to medium-high and cook, stirring frequently, until the shrimps turn pink, about 5 minutes. Stir in the cream and Pernod, if using, and bring to a boil. Reduce the heat to low and simmer, covered, for 10 minutes. Add the clams and mussels to the sauce and cook for 1 minute, just until heated through.

Divide the spaghetti among 4 plates. Remove the artichoke hearts, mussels, and shrimps from the sauce. Return the mussels to the reserved half shells. Spoon sauce over the spaghetti and top each plate with 3 artichoke hearts, 3 mussels, and 1 shrimp. Garnish with celery leaves, if desired.

= Robert Mondavi Winery Stag's Leap District Sauvignon Blanc

MARY WILSON

This is a perfect meal for bachelors and bachelorettes because the uneaten portions can be stored in the fridge for later. I also recommend that you eat it on New Year's Day for good luck. It's a Southern tradition.

☆

Mary Wilson, co-founder of the Supremes, has an unequaled record of Number One hits. She has never stopped touring and developing new projects and entertaining her fans. Ms. Wilson has done extensive charity work, raising millions for AIDS. She also works to raise funds for the homeless, cancer research, and victims of child abuse.

RICHARD ARMAS

Supremely Healthy Turkey and Black-eyed Peas with Couscous

3 tablespoons oil

1 medium onion, chopped

2 garlic cloves, minced

Chopped cilantro, to taste

4 small turkey drumsticks or wings

1 pound dried black-eyed peas, soaked overnight and drained

1 pound carrots, chopped

1 pound celery, chopped

Pinch of garlic powder

Pinch of black pepper

Pinch of cayenne

3 tablespoons flour or 1 tablespoon cornstarch (optional)

Couscous (recipe follows)

Heat the oil in a large skillet. Add the onion, garlic, and cilantro. Add the turkey parts and brown them. Add the black-eyed peas and cover with water. Cook for 1 hour, or until the peas are tender. Add the carrots, celery, garlic powder, pepper, and cayenne and continue to cook until the vegetables are tender, about 20 minutes. If desired, thicken with flour or cornstarch. Serve with couscous.

Couscous

(Serves 4)

1 chicken bouillon cube

1 garlic clove, minced

Salt, to taste

2 cups couscous
Olive oil
Lemon juice, to taste

Bring 4 cups of water to boil. Add the bouillon cube, garlic, salt, and couscous. Cover and remove from heat. Let steam for 20 minutes. Add olive oil and lemon juice to taste.

=*Robert Mondavi Winery Napa Valley Fumé Blanc*

Side Dishes

LEE GRANT

Lee Grant made her stage debut at the age of four in a Metropolitan Opera production. At eleven she became a member of the American Ballet and at fourteen, after graduating from high school, she won a scholarship to the Neighborhood Playhouse. She played a shoplifter in *Detective Story* on Broadway and repeated the role in the film version. She won a Critics Circle award for the stage version and was nominated for an Oscar and won the Best Actress Award at the Cannes Film Festival for the film version. Immediately after this she was blacklisted when she refused to testify against her then-husband, Arnold Manoff, before the House Un-American Activities Committee. She continued to appear on stage and has returned to the big screen in a variety of noteworthy roles. She won the Oscar for best supporting actress for *Shampoo* and Emmy awards for "Peyton Place" and "Neon Ceiling."

LEE GRANT

Steamed Cabbage

(Serves 4 to 6)

1 head cabbage, quartered and cored
1 teaspoon salt
¼ cup extra virgin olive oil
½ teaspoon crushed red pepper
2 cups cooked sliced carrots, chopped cauliflower, torn spinach leaves, or baby new potatoes

Separate the cabbage leaves by hand, sprinkle with salt, and wash well. Using your hands, coat each leaf with oil. Place in a large skillet, add red pepper and 1 cup water, cover, and steam over medium heat for 1½ hours. Check every 30 minutes and add water as needed. Cabbage is done when it has a whitish translucent look. At this point, combine it with the other vegetables and serve.

Applesauce

(Serves 4 to 6)

6 Granny Smith apples, cored, peeled, and quartered
6 McIntosh apples, cored, peeled, and quartered
½ cup water
1 teaspoon ground cinnamon, nutmeg, or pumpkin pie spice

Combine all the ingredients in a saucepan and cook over low heat for 30 minutes, or until done. The sauce will be chunky. Serve with lamb, chicken, or pork.

= *Vichon Chevrignon*

LYNN TANNER

LYNN TANNER

The rum pot recipe is intensely charged, and it strengthens with time. As in a theatrical ensemble, you take the proper ingredients, mix them together, pray for time for the results to ripen, and—voila!—a successful project. Enjoy, but get your designated driver ready!

Lynn Tanner, a bright and vivacious actress, does it all: stage, screen, TV, writing, producing. Her big-screen films include *Damage*, *Twisted*, and *Another Time, Another Place*; TV movies include *Finding Your Way Home* and *Waiting for the Parade*. She has gained critical acclaim for her stage performances in Gardner McKay's *Toyer*, Steve Allen's *The Wake*, *Marvin's Room*, and *The Gingerbread Lady*. Ms. Tanner is currently working on three screenplays: *Gilul*, *Tessa Deare*, and *Reasons*. Despite all this work, she still finds time to contribute to our cause.

Rum Pot

Small scale to weigh fruit and sugar
Large glass jar or crockery pot with a lid, washed with hot soapy water, rinsed, and dried

Any combination of the following fruit
Pineapple, peeled, cored, eyes cut out, and cut into large chunks
Peaches, peeled by dropping in boiling water for a moment first, and pitted if desired
Plums, peeled the same way as peaches and pitted if desired
Apricots, peeled the same way as peaches and pitted if desired
Strawberries, hulled and washed
Cherries, stems removed, washed, and pits left in
Dried apricots (optional)

Dark rum to cover fruit by ½ inch

Weigh the fruit and weigh out an equal amount of sugar. Place both sugar and fruit in the jar or crockery pot and cover with dark rum. Rum should come to about ½ inch above the fruit. (Fruit may float for a few days.) Tightly screw the lid on the jar and label it with the date. Leave in a cool, dark place for 10 to 12 weeks. It will last for years.

Replenish the rum pot every time you take something out. Add an equal weight of sugar and fruit. Keep the rum ½ inch above the fruit, adding more rum when it goes below that. Heat the fruit compote to serve with meat or use it as is as a topping for crepes, ice cream, or pound cake.

=*Robert Mondavi Winery Moscato d'Oro*

AUDREY MEADOWS

Audrey Meadows was a successful performer on Broadway and on television before joining "The Honeymooners" as Alice Kramden, but it was "The Jackie Gleason Show" that earned her an Emmy. She starred in many other TV programs and films and continued to appear frequently in television roles until her death in 1995.

☆

Audrey used to make this recipe when she was at her ranch in Colorado. It's really a Szechuan dish. The trick is to remember to remove the cubed eggplant from the marinade. Audrey once forgot, put it all in together, and cooked the gravy away.

To My friend Paul, "Continued success" Best always
Audrey Meadows

Lazy Six Japanese Eggplant

(Serves 6 to 8)

5 to 6 medium eggplants, cubed
¼ cup soy sauce
¼ cup vinegar
2 tablespoons sugar
1 tablespoon chopped fresh ginger
1 tablespoon chopped garlic
2 tablespoons chopped scallion, including green tops
½ teaspoon chili paste with garlic or black bean sauce
1 to 2 tablespoons peanut oil

Marinate the eggplant in all of the remaining ingredients, except the peanut oil, for 15 to 20 minutes. Remove the eggplant from the marinade and sauté in hot peanut oil. When partly done, add 2 tablespoons water. Cover and steam for 3 to 5 minutes. Add the marinade and simmer until reduced to a thin gravy. Don't cook away all the gravy!

 =Woodbridge White Zinfandel

JAMES CROMWELL

JAMES CROMWELL

Besides stage, TV, and film acting, James (Jamie) Cromwell is an occasional cartoonist; he is currently working on a science-fiction novel dealing with the Roswell incident. Since he started in television in 1974 and films in 1976, he has had more than sixty appearances. He was nominated for an Academy Award for *Babe*. Other major films include *Deep Impact*, *Species II*, and *Star Trek: First Contact*.

Jamie Cromwell

Sautéed Kale with Garlic and Bread Crumbs

(Serves 4)

1 tablespoon olive oil
¼ cup Italian-style bread crumbs
1 tablespoon minced garlic
⅛ teaspoon salt
1 large bunch of kale, rinsed and stems and tough ribs removed

Heat the olive oil in a large skillet, add the bread crumbs, garlic, and salt, and sauté for 2 minutes. Add the kale, turning with tongs. Sauté for 2 minutes more, or just until the leaves wilt.

= *Robert Mondavi Winery Napa Valley Fumé Blanc*

LEE MERIWETHER

I risk animosity from my daughters, Kyle and Lesley, for giving away Sweet Potato Mellow Crisp because it has become their very own and has been loved and asked for by their friends. But when I told them that their favorite Thanksgiving side dish would help to raise funds for AIDS education and research, they were happy and thrilled to part with "their" recipe.

☆

Lee Meriwether, a former Miss San Francisco, Miss California, and Miss America, is probably known to most people as Betty in the TV series "Barnaby Jones," co-starring Buddy Ebsen. The show ran for eight very successful years. She has been in many different series including "The Time Tunnel," "Mission: Impossible," and "Dr. Kildare." Some of her memorable film roles were as Catwoman in the original *Batman, Angel in My Pocket* and *The Undefeated*. Live theater continues to be her first love and she has enjoyed working with her daughters, Kyle and Lesley, in such productions as *The Gingerbread Lady* and *It's a Wonderful World*. Lee is active in numerous charities, such as the International Society for Crippled Children, Women in Show Business (an organization that funds reconstructive surgery for needy children), the Cystic Fibrosis Foundation, and the Blind Children's Center. She has long been associated with animal rights groups.

LEE MERIWETHER

Kyle and Lesley's Sweet Potato Mellow Crisp

(Serves 6)

2 cans (15¾ ounces each) yams
¼ cup orange juice
¾ cup flour
½ cup sugar
1 teaspoon cinnamon
Dash of salt
¼ pound (1 stick) margarine or butter
1½ cups miniature marshmallows

Place the yams in a 10 × 6-inch shallow baking dish and pour the orange juice over. Combine the flour, sugar, cinnamon, and salt in a bowl and mix well. Cut in the margarine (or butter) until the mixture resembles coarse crumbs. Sprinkle over the yams. Bake at 350 degrees for 30 minutes. Sprinkle marshmallows on top. Put under the broiler until light brown, watching every second.

= *Robert Mondavi Winery Moscato d'Oro*

DEAN JONES

Leading man of Hollywood films, Dean Jones is often seen in Disney features. A former blues singer, he has starred in the TV series "Ensign O'Toole." He also appeared on Broadway in the hit musical *Company*. His films include *The Love Bug* and *The Shaggy D.A.*

Southern Corn Bread

(Serves 4 to 6)

¼ cup shortening
2 cups white cornmeal
2 tablespoons all-purpose flour
2 tablespoons baking powder
1 teaspoon baking soda
1 teaspoon salt
2 cups buttermilk
1 egg, lightly beaten

*M*elt the shortening in a 9-inch cast-iron skillet or 9-inch square baking pan, brushing the sides of the pan with melted shortening. Sift together the dry ingredients. Combine the buttermilk and egg and stir in the dry ingredients and the melted shortening. Pour into the skillet or pan. Bake at 450 degrees for 20 to 25 minutes.

Tip: You might try this for extra flavor: Cut about 4 slices of bacon into bits, fry until crisp, and stir into the mixture, fat and all.

When cold, the corn bread can be split in half, cut in squares, and served with creamed chicken between the slices and over the top. Sprinkle with fresh parsley.

 = Robert Mondavi Napa Valley Pinot Noir

BETTY FORD

Warm or cold, buttered or unbuttered, this favorite of the Ford family always appears at holiday gatherings.

☆

As our First Lady from 1974 to 1977, Betty Ford spoke her mind on controversial issues and campaigned for the adoption of the Equal Rights Amendment. She was greatly admired for her honesty and openness. Mrs. Ford has received many awards for her work in support of the arts and for helping handicapped and retarded children. After leaving the White House, she founded the Betty Ford Center in Rancho Mirage, California, to help others with addictions to drugs and alcohol. She has also coauthored (with Chris Chase) two books, *Times of My Life* and *Betty: A Glad Awakening.*

BETTY FORD

Blu' Bana Bread

(Makes 2 loaves)

½ pound (2 sticks) butter
2 cups sugar
4 eggs
2 teaspoons vanilla extract
5 ripe bananas, mashed
4 cups sifted all-purpose flour
3 teaspoons allspice
2 teaspoons baking soda
1 teaspoon baking powder
½ teaspoon salt
2 cups fresh or frozen blueberries, drained

Grease and flour two 9 × 5–inch loaf pans. Cream together the butter and sugar. Beat in the eggs, then add the vanilla. Fold in mashed bananas and 2 cups of the flour. Set aside 2 tablespoons of the remaining flour. Place the rest in a sifter and add the allspice, baking soda, baking powder, and salt. Sift and fold into the banana mixture. Sprinkle the blueberries with the reserved flour, coating well, and fold into the batter. Divide the batter between the loaf pans. Bake at 325 degrees for about 50 minutes. Test with a toothpick to determine when bread is done.

= Robert Mondavi Winery Moscato d'Oro

KATHIE LEE AND FRANK GIFFORD

Kathie Lee Gifford is a woman of the Nineties, an entertainer, businesswoman, wife, and mother. As co-host of the popular morning talk show "Live with Regis & Kathie Lee," she shares her secrets for surviving with millions of viewers. She began her professional singing career at fourteen, with a folk group called Pennsylvania Next Right. At seventeen she won Maryland's Junior Miss title, and at twenty she was off to Hollywood. While a regular on "Days of Our Lives" she played a character known as Nurse Callahan. In 1977 Kathie Lee became a featured singer on the game show "Name That Tune." Later the producers of "Good Morning America" offered her a job as a substitute anchor for Joan Lunden. Despite their busy schedules, Kathie Lee and her husband, Frank Gifford, devote a great deal of time to numerous charities. Two of these are Cody's House and Cassidy's Place, facilities that provide shelter and care to HIV-positive and crack-addicted children.

DANA FINEMAN/SYGMA

God Bless You!
Kathie Lee Gifford

Best Wishes
Frank Gifford

Apple-Bran Muffins

(Makes 12 muffins)

1 cup all-purpose flour
1½ tablespoons baking powder
2 teaspoons baking soda
¼ teaspoon salt
1 teaspoon ground cinnamon
¾ cup sugar
¾ cup bran flake cereal
½ cup milk
1 large egg
⅓ cup vegetable oil
½ cup orange juice
1 cup peeled, cored, and diced green apple
Butter or vegetable oil cooking spray, for greasing muffin cups

Sift together the flour, baking powder, baking soda, salt, cinnamon, and sugar. Add the bran cereal and mix. Beat together the milk, egg, oil, and orange juice. Stir in the apple. Pour the liquid mixture into the dry mixture and stir to combine. Do not beat. Grease 12 standard-size muffin cups with butter or spray. Spoon the batter into the cups, filling three quarters full. Bake at 350 degrees for 20 minutes. Remove muffins from pans and set on racks to cool.

Frank Gifford entered the Pro Football Hall of Fame in recognition of his many years as a record-setting player. Since beginning his broadcasting career while still an active New York Giants player, he has hosted ABC's "Wide World of Sports" and anchored seven Olympic Games and five Super Bowl Games. For over twenty-five years he has served as a member of ABC's award-winning Monday night NFL broadcast team. Since 1957 he has not only been one of our most indispensable sportscasters but has done it with a style all his own.

ANGELA LANSBURY

I have always found the making of bread to be the most relaxing thing in the world. When I was on the road with shows, I would take a hotel suite with a kitchen and bake my own bread as usual. This particular recipe is my favorite; it goes well with cheese or jam.

☆

Angela Lansbury is one of the hardest-working and most professional actresses around. She won an Oscar nomination for her first Hollywood role in *Gaslight* and two more for *The Picture of Dorian Gray* and *The Manchurian Candidate*. Ms. Lansbury is a four-time Tony winner and has achieved TV superstardom at 70 with her hit series "Murder, She Wrote."

ANGELA LANSBURY

Famous Power Loaf

(Makes 2 loaves)

2 cups boiling water
1 ½ cups cracked wheat cereal
3 tablespoons shortening
2 tablespoons honey
1 tablespoon salt
2 envelopes dry active yeast
⅔ cup warm water (105 to 115 degrees)
4 cups stone-ground whole wheat flour
2 handfuls of bran flakes
2 handfuls of quick-cooking oats
½ cup wheat germ

Pour boiling water over the cracked wheat cereal and stir it. Add the shortening, honey, and salt to the cereal. Set the mixture aside to cool to lukewarm.

Dissolve the yeast in the warm water and add it to the cereal mixture. Gradually stir in 3 cups of the whole wheat flour, then stir in the bran flakes, oats, and wheat germ. Mix all the ingredients very well and cover the bowl with a damp cloth. Let the dough rise until it has doubled in bulk. That takes about 1 hour to 1 hour 15 minutes, so I sometimes start the dough, then go out to garden while it's rising.

When the dough has risen, divide the dough in half and place on a baking sheet or in 2 loaf pans. Bake at 350 degrees for 45 minutes, or until nicely browned.

= *Robert Mondavi Winery Napa Valley Moscato d'Oro*

PATTY LOVELESS

Patty Loveless has accomplished much in her career. She is only the second woman in history to win the Country Music Academy Award for Album of the Year. She has gold and platinum albums to her credit. Ms. Loveless captivates her audience by just stepping on stage and unleashing her voice.

RANDEE ST. NICHOLAS

Cranberry Nut Bread

(Makes 1 large or 2 small loaves)

¼ pound (1 stick) butter, softened
¾ cup sugar
1 egg
2½ cups all-purpose flour
1 tablespoon baking powder
1 teaspoon salt
⅔ cup orange juice
1 teaspoon grated orange zest
⅓ cup milk
¾ cup chopped fresh or frozen cranberries
½ cup chopped pecans

Cream the butter and sugar in a large mixing bowl until fluffy. Beat in the egg. Stir together the flour, baking powder, and salt in a separate bowl. Combine the orange juice, orange zest, and milk in a separate container. Add alternately with the dry ingredients to the creamed mixture, mixing after each addition. Fold in the cranberries and half the pecans. Pour into 1 greased 8½ × 4½ × 2½-inch loaf pan or 2 greased 7½ × 3½ × 2-inch loaf pans. Sprinkle with the remaining pecans. Bake at 350 degrees for about 60 minutes for a large pan or 45 to 50 minutes for the small pans. Cool loaves in pans for 10 minutes, then remove from pans. Cool completely.

=*Robert Mondavi Winery Napa Valley Moscato d'Oro*

NANCY REAGAN

Nancy Reagan, former First Lady and wife of one of the most popular presidents we've ever had, brought style and grace to the White House. She still devotes much of her time to humanitarian causes. The name of her recipe is somewhat incongruous with her personal elegance— Monkey Bread.

Monkey Bread

(Makes 2 Loaves)

1 package active dry yeast
1 to 1¼ cups milk, lukewarm
3 eggs
3 tablespoons sugar
1 teaspoon salt
3½ cups all-purpose flour
6 ounces (1½ sticks) butter, at room temperature
½ pound (2 sticks) butter, melted

Mix the yeast with some of the milk in a bowl until dissolved. Add two of the eggs and beat. Mix in the sugar, salt, and flour. Add the remaining milk, a little at a time, mixing thoroughly. Cut in the butter until blended. Knead the dough, then let rise for 1 to 1 ½ hours, or until double in size. Knead again and let rise for 40 minutes.

Roll out the dough on a floured board and shape into a log. Cut the log into 28 pieces of equal size. Shape each piece of dough into a ball and roll in melted butter. Butter and flour two 9-inch ring molds. Place 7 balls in each mold, leaving spaces in between. Place the remaining balls on top, spacing evenly. Let the dough rise to the top of the molds. Beat the remaining egg and brush the tops with it. Bake at 375 degrees for about 15 minutes, or until golden brown.

 *=La Famiglia Tocai Friulano*

ASHLEY JUDD

Ashley Judd did not need to cash in on her mother's or her sister's fame to build a solid reputation for herself. She had good roles in good movies like *Smoke* and *A Time to Kill* with Matthew McConaughey. She also appeared on HBO's "Norma Jean and Marilyn" and *Kiss the Girls* with Morgan Freeman. Ashley graduated with honors from the University of Kentucky. She counts food, sex, books, and God among her passions (not necessarily in that order)!

THE JUDDS

Perfect Biscuits

(Makes about 20 biscuits)

2 cups self-rising flour
¼ cup shortening or lard
⅞ cup nonfat milk

Sift the flour and cut in the shortening with your fingers until the mixture is like coarse beads. Make a well in the middle of the flour and pour the milk into the well. Using your index fingers, stir the flour and milk together, letting the dough collect into a small ball. Pat out on a floured surface, about ½ inch thick. Cut into biscuits. Bake at 450 degrees for 10 to 15 minutes.

Tips: Do not overwork the dough; the less you handle it, the softer and lighter your biscuits will be. The exact quantity of milk is important. Tammy Wynette taught me to use about ⅞ of a cup.

 *= Woodbridge Chardonnay*

STAR JONES

Old-fashioned sweet pie that will taste out of this world!

☆

Star Jones, co-host of television's "The View," is a lawyer and former prosecutor. She is best known for her candor, confidence, and uncanny ability to clarify muddy legal issues. Her knowledge of the law and talent for television have won her critical acclaim as a news correspondent.

Enjoy The View!

ABC PHOTO, ANDREW ECCLES

Sweet Potato Pie

(Makes 2 pies)

2 large sweet potatoes, scrubbed
½ pound (2 sticks) butter, at room temperature
4 eggs
2 cups sugar, or to taste
1 can (8 ounces) evaporated milk
4 tablespoons nutmeg
4 tablespoons cinnamon
2 tablespoons vanilla extract
1 teaspoon flour
Two 9-inch pie crusts

Boil the sweet potatoes until soft. Peel and mash the potatoes with the butter in a large mixing bowl until all the lumps are removed. Add the eggs, one at a time, mixing after each egg. Add the sugar, nutmeg, and cinnamon, mixing after each spice is added. Add the vanilla and flour. Mix until smooth. Pour into the pie crusts. Bake at 350 degrees for 1½ hours, or until the crust is golden brown.

 =*La Famiglia Malvasia Bianca*

CARYL AND MARILYN

Artery Bread is one of the first things Marilyn and I bonded over. She is an awesome chef and this is my favorite of all her recipes. It's about as decadent as you can get! I named it Artery Bread because there is so much butter and cream and cheese in it that you can feel your arteries closing on you, but look at it this way, if you die, you die very happy! —Caryl Kristensen

☆

I was inspired by a trip to the Garlic Festival in Gilroy, California, back in 1982. There I experienced tastes and smells and tourists that were not of this world. That year, the winning recipe was a creamy garlic French bread. I added parmesan cheese, thicker cream, butter, more spices, and many more calories to create a bread for which the Surgeon General should post a warning. When Caryl tasted it she gave it the name Artery Bread.
—Marilyn Kentz

CARYL AND MARILYN

Marilyn Kentz

Caryl Kristensen

Artery Bread

(Makes 1 loaf)

1 long sourdough baguette
5 garlic cloves, finely chopped
¼ pound (1 stick) salted butter
2 cups heavy cream
1 cup grated parmesan cheese, not freshly grated, or more to taste
2 tablespoons ground coriander
Pepper medley, to taste
Parsley flakes, to taste
Your favorite spices, to taste

Melt about 2 tablespoons or less of the butter in a medium saucepan. Add the garlic and sauté until golden. Slice the baguette the length of the bread, creating 2 halves. Then cut 3-inch-wide slices down each half, without cutting all the way through to the bottom. Add the remaining butter to the saucepan and melt it. Evenly pour the garlic and butter over each half of the bread. Set the saucepan aside, but don't clean it yet. Close the bread back up and put it on a baking sheet. Bake, uncovered, until the outside is slightly crispy and the inside is very warm.

Caryl Kristensen and Marilyn Kentz became friends in the late Eighties. Their sense of humor meshed, so they decided to put together a live comedy show. The result, "Comedy Camp for Mommies," was hilarious, and comedy clubs were selling out the show months in advance everywhere they were booked. Caryl and Marilyn delighted television fans with two seasons of "The Mommies" followed by their talk show, "Caryl and Marilyn, Real Friends." They recently wrote a book, *The Motherload: When Your Life's on Spin Cycle and You Just Can't Get the Lid Up*, which is available in bookstores now.

While the bread is heating, pour the cream into the buttery saucepan and add the parmesan cheese and the rest of the ingredients. Stir slowly until the sauce is thick and rich. This may take 15 minutes or so. You can add more cheese to help thicken the cream at any time. When the bread is warm and sauce is ready, open the bread back up and begin to pour the sauce over it. This may need 2 people to get the sauce into the cracks between the slices: one to pour and the other to use 2 forks to open the cracks up. Choose the second person carefully: You don't want someone who can't control her drooling! The cream should be all over the bread and the baking sheet. You will need a knife and spatula to serve the Artery Bread. Also be ready to wipe the brows of your guests; they will be in heaven.

Tip: Do not schedule a cholesterol check within a week of eating this bread.

 =Robert Mondavi Winery Napa Valley Chardonnay

Desserts

GEORGE HAMILTON

GEORGE HAMILTON

George Hamilton, the tanned and handsome star of films and television, is renowned for his roles in "Dynasty"; *The Godfather, Part III; Zorro, the Gay Blade;* and *Love at First Bite.* George has parlayed his sun worshipping into a line of skin care products and the George Hamilton Sun Care System. He also owns Hamilton's: A Wine Bar, a purveyor of fine wines and cigars. You can catch him in the new daytime TV series "The Guilt."

Chocolate Chip Cookies

(Makes 3 dozen cookies)

½ cup shortening
¼ cup (packed) brown sugar
½ cup granulated sugar
1 egg
1 teaspoon vanilla extract
1 cup sifted all-purpose flour
¾ teaspoon salt
½ teaspoon baking soda
1 package (6 ounces) semisweet chocolate pieces (1 cup)
½ cup broken nuts

Cream the shortening, brown sugar, and granulated sugar. Beat in the egg and vanilla until light and fluffy. Sift together the flour, salt, and baking soda and stir into the creamed mixture. Fold in the chocolate and nuts. Drop from a teaspoon 2 inches apart on a greased baking sheet. Bake at 350 degrees for 10 to 12 minutes. Remove immediately.

 = Robert Mondavi Winery Moscato d'Oro

LADY BIRD JOHNSON

Claudia (Lady Bird) Johnson was First Lady of the United States from 1963 to 1969. She had always been a proponent of conservation, and during her tenure as First Lady she began the National Beautification Project and a campaign for the conservation of our nation's wildflowers. As a result, as you drive along today's highways your spirits may be lifted by brightly colored wildflowers growing in profusion where none had been before. Mrs. Johnson also made many parks in our nation's capital more user friendly.

S. M. SCHONBRUNN

Mrs. Lyndon B. Johnson

Lace Cookies

(Makes 3 dozen cookies)

1 cup flour
½ cup sweetened flaked coconut
¼ cup corn syrup, light or dark
¼ cup (packed) brown sugar
4 tablespoons (½ stick) margarine
½ teaspoon vanilla extract

Mix the flour with the coconut. Mix the corn syrup, brown sugar, and margarine in a saucepan until well blended and cook over medium heat, stirring constantly. Remove from the heat and stir in the vanilla. Gradually blend in the flour mixture. Drop by the teaspoonful 3 to 4 inches apart on an ungreased baking sheet. Bake at 325 degrees for 12 to 15 minutes, or until the edges are lightly browned.

Tip: Lace cookies are served alone or with fresh peach ice cream at the ranch. They're also perfect for that special tea or brunch.

=*Robert Mondavi Napa Valley Moscato d'Oro*

JACKIE COLLINS

JACKIE COLLINS

Jackie Collins is one of the world's top-selling writers, with two hundred million copies of her books sold in more than forty countries. Her sixteen best-selling novels have never been out of print. Among those that were made into movies or television miniseries are *Hollywood Wives, Lucky, Lady Boss: A Novel, Chances, The Stud, Yesterday's Hero,* and *The Bitch.* Her hobbies include exploring exotic locations, photography, and soul music.

Orange Chocolate Cheesecake

(Makes 1 cake)

2 packages milk chocolate cookies
½ pound (2 sticks) butter
1½ tubs (12 ounces each) whipped cream cheese
1 cup sugar
3 teaspoons orange extract
½ cup finely grated orange zest
¼ pound (1 stick) butter, softened
2 eggs, lightly beaten
½ cup heavy cream
1 cup sour cream

Melt one stick of the butter and mix with the cookies to make a paste. Press into the bottom of a large square baking dish. Bake at 450 degrees for 5 minutes. Let cool.

Mix the cream cheese, ¾ cup of the sugar, 2 teaspoons of the orange extract, half of the grated orange zest, one stick of softened butter, the eggs, and half of the cream. Pour over the crust and bake at 350 degrees for 20 minutes. Let cool.

Mix the sour cream, the remaining 1 teaspoon orange extract, and ¼ cup of sugar, then pour over the cake. Bake for 5 minutes and let cool. Sprinkle the remaining grated orange zest on top of the cake.

= Robert Mondavi Winery Moscato d'Oro

GARRETT GLASER

CNBC

Garrett Glaser, formerly a correspondent for "Entertainment Tonight," has written articles on media for the *Los Angeles Times*, the *Advocate*, and *Electronic Media*. He won an Emmy for Individual Achievement in News Reporting and an Associated Press Broadcasters Award for Best Local Newscast. Mr. Glaser reports on the business of popular culture, trends, and advertising for CNBC.

Aunt Emma's New England Rice Pudding

(Serves 6)

1½ cups boiled rice
6 eggs beaten with ¾ cup sugar
1 teaspoon vanilla extract
5 cups whole milk
Handful of raisins
Cinnamon and nutmeg, to taste

Toss all the ingredients together in a glass ovenproof bowl. Place the bowl in a shallow pan with ½ inch of boiling water. Bake at 325 degrees for 1 hour 15 minutes or so. Sprinkle more cinnamon and nutmeg on top. Mmmmmmmmmmm!

 =Robert Mondavi Napa Valley Moscato d'Oro

ROLONDA WATTS

Less than a year after saying good-bye to her syndicated talk show, Rolonda Watts was back, this time fulfilling her lifelong dream of acting and performing, in her role as the vivacious vixen Vivica on WB's "Sister, Sister." What many do not know is that Rolonda holds a degree in theater arts with a specialty in comedy from Spelman College. "I'm a firm believer that life should be gulped, not sipped," says Rolonda. Her other accomplishments include anchoring for "Inside Edition." She has appeared in Spike Lee's *Girl 6* as well as several impressive theater productions and has been nominated for both an Emmy and a Cable Ace Award. She has also received the NAACP Image Award and a UNCF Award. Whether as an actress, reporter, anchor, producer, or senior correspondent, Rolonda Watts has had an impact on viewing audiences of all ages and backgrounds.

MARC RABOY

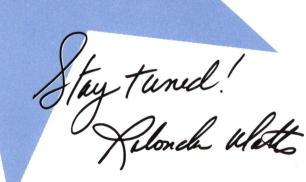

Stay tuned!
Rolonda Watts

Rolonda's Shakin' Quakin' Apple Cakin'

(Serves 10)

½ cup maple syrup

4 tablespoons (½ stick) margarine or butter, melted

1 teaspoon cinnamon

2½ apples, peeled, cored, and sliced

1½ cups all-purpose flour

2 teaspoons baking powder

¼ teaspoon salt

4 tablespoons (½ stick) margarine or butter, softened

1 cup sugar

1 egg

1 teaspoon vanilla extract

¾ cup milk

Mix the syrup, melted margarine, and cinnamon in a greased 9-inch square baking pan. Arrange the apples over syrup mixture. Mix the flour, baking powder, and salt in small bowl. Beat the softened margarine and sugar in a large bowl with an electric mixer on medium speed until light and fluffy. Beat in the egg and vanilla. Add the flour mixture alternately with the milk, beating well after each addition until smooth. Pour over the apples. Bake at 350 degrees for 45 to 50 minutes, or until a toothpick inserted in the center comes out clean. Cool for 5 minutes. Loosen the edges of the cake from the side of the pan and invert onto a serving plate.

 = Vichon Sémillon Botrytis

GERALDO RIVERA

Geraldo Rivera began his career in 1970 as a reporter for "Eyewitness News." He is an award-winning investigative reporter and one of America's best known television journalists. He is an accomplished author, news producer, and talk-show host. His numerous contributions in broadcasting have made him a force to be reckoned with. He supports many charities, including the Maravilla Foundation, Working Organization for Retarded Children and Adults, and the Geraldo Rivera Golf and Tennis Classic. Proceeds from the latter go to building homes for mentally and developmentally challenged people. Geraldo truly believes in helping those in need.

GERALDO RIVERA

Amaretto Caramel Custard

FLAN CON AMARETTO

(Serves 8 to 10)

1 cup sugar
1 can (14 ounces) sweetened condensed milk
1 large can (12 ounces) evaporated milk
4 large eggs
1 cup water
½ cup amaretto

Put the sugar in the top of a double boiler over medium heat. Stir until melted. Do not burn. Let the caramel cool. Mix all the other ingredients and place in the caramel pan in the double boiler. Cook until a knife comes out clean. Cool, then refrigerate for 2 hours before serving.

Note: Recipe written for Geraldo by Hilda Rodriguez.

=*Robert Mondavi Napa Valley Sauvignon Blanc Botrytis*

MAUREEN MCGOVERN

I lived in New York City for eighteen years and had a copy of every take-out menu on the Upper West Side of Manhattan! Since culinary skills do not rank among my strengths (nor do I have a lot of free time), I always look for easy, quick, nutritional recipes for healthy eating. This recipe satisfies the sweet tooth and is relatively low in fat. For less fat use a light oil.

☆

Maureen McGovern is a singer of unparalleled purity of vocal range. Her talent encompasses the Broadway stage, recordings, television, concerts, films, and radio. Her career began with the Number One gold record "The Morning After," which won an Academy Award for Best Song from *The Poseidon Adventure*. She received a second Oscar for "We May Never Love Like This Again" from *The Towering Inferno*. Aside from her busy performance schedule, Maureen supports a number of charities. She serves as Vice-President and National Chairperson of the Polymyositis/Dermatomyositis division of the Muscular Dystrophy Association (MDA). She has performed on the "Jerry Lewis MDA Telethon" for the past seventeen years.

Maureen McGovern

Fresh Fruit Cobbler

(Serves 6)

2 cups blueberries

6 to 8 fresh peaches, peeled, pitted, and sliced

½ cup raisins

¼ cup apple, apricot, or peach juice

1 teaspoon cinnamon

1 cup rolled oats

½ cup chopped almonds

2 tablespoons sesame seeds

¼ cup sunflower seeds

4 tablespoons safflower oil

Nutmeg, to taste

Combine the blueberries, peaches, raisins, and juice. Spoon into a greased 13 × 9–inch baking dish. Sprinkle with cinnamon. Mix the oats, almonds, and seeds in a bowl. Add the oil and blend with a fork. Sprinkle over the fruit, then sprinkle with nutmeg. Bake at 350 degrees for 1 hour.

= *Robert Mondavi Napa Valley Moscato Bianco*

SALLY JESSY RAPHAËL

If I am in a strange city standing on a street corner, I'm the one people ask for directions. If I'm in a restaurant ladies' room, the woman next to me tells me her life story!

☆

Sally Jessy Raphaël is the kind of person people like to confide in. They seem to sense that she will understand their problems, and more often than not she does. Success didn't come easily to her but after many difficult years she's finally come into her own with "The Sally Jessy Raphaël Show." Sally isn't content just to sit back and enjoy her success; she also gives of herself to a number of charitable causes, including the Pediatric AIDS Foundation and the National Head Injury Foundation. As if her life weren't already filled to capacity, she also finds time to run her own bed and breakfast, the Isaac Stover House in Bucks County, Pennsylvania.

STUDIOS USA TELEVISION DISTRIBUTION LLC.

love ♡

Sally J. Raphaël

Sally's Oatmeal Cookies

(Makes 4 dozen cookies)

3 cups sifted all-purpose flour
1 teaspoon baking soda
1 teaspoon salt
1 teaspoon cinnamon
3 cups old-fashioned oatmeal
1 cup granulated sugar
1 cup (packed) dark brown sugar
1 cup raisins
1 cup vegetable oil
2 eggs
⅓ cup milk

Place 2 oven racks in the oven. Line 2 baking sheets with aluminum foil. Sift the flour, baking soda, salt, and cinnamon into a very large mixing bowl. Mix the oatmeal, granulated sugar, brown sugar, raisins, oil, eggs, and milk. Add to the flour mixture, mixing until the ingredients are well combined. Drop the batter in rounded tablespoons, the size of a walnut, onto the baking sheets. Bake at 375 degrees for 15 to 20 minutes, reversing the baking sheets once halfway through the cooking time. If the cookie bottoms are burning, place another baking sheet underneath and bake the next batch 1 sheet at a time. Remove the cookies to a rack to cool.

=*Robert Mondavi Napa Valley Moscato d'Oro*

NELY GALAN

NELY GALAN

As President and CEO of Galan Entertainment, founded in 1994, Nely Galan oversees a multifaceted entertainment company dedicated to producing and marketing Latino-themed media properties for companies with interests in the U.S. Latino and Latin American markets. Her unique blend of creativity, business savvy, and financial acumen have made her one of the most successful businesswomen in Hollywood.

Custard Cake

(Serves 10)

3 cups milk
1 cinnamon stick
Zest of 1 lime, removed in strips
¼ teaspoon salt
7 egg yolks
1½ cups sugar
4½ tablespoons cornstarch dissolved in ¼ cup water
1 can (12 ounces) evaporated milk
3 tablespoons Triple Sec Liquor
1 package Ladyfingers Soft cake mix, prepared according to package directions

Boil the milk with the cinnamon stick, lime zest, and salt. Strain and let cool. Beat the egg yolks with sugar and cornstarch dissolved in water. Add the infused milk and evaporated milk. Cook at medium heat, stirring constantly, until thick. Add the Triple Sec. Let cool. Alternate a layer of custard and a layer of cake. Place in refrigerator.

Custard Cake is one of my favorite recipes. The delicious smells take me back to my childhood in Cuba, watching my mother fix my dinner and learning how to prepare the recipe myself. The recipe and the memories have stayed with me all my life, and I am happy to share it with you now. Fix yourself a little cafecito (Cuban coffee) after the perfect meal, and you too will enjoy a bit of Cuba in your kitchen.

 =Robert Mondavi Winery Moscato d'Oro

NOLAN MILLER

Many times over the years I have been a guest at the Evergreens Plantation near New Orleans. The food is always delicious. The hush puppies, pecan pie, the homemade fresh peach ice cream—but it's the bananas that I always look forward to!

☆

Nolan Miller has created some of the world's most glamorous fashions. He has spent over thirty years working in film, theater, and television as a costume designer and has designed for such shows as "Dynasty," a show as famous for its fashions as its plot or characters. Since 1992 he has become more visible, with one of QVC's top costume jewelry shows—"The Nolan Miller Glamour Collection." Mr. Miller has worked with some of the most famous women in the world, who have worn his designs both on- and off-screen. They include Elizabeth Taylor, Barbara Stanwyck, Sophia Loren, Linda Evans, and Joan Collins.

Nolan Miller

NOLAN MILLER

Southern Plantation Bananas

(Serves 8)

½ cup (packed) brown sugar
4 tablespoons (½ stick) butter
4 bananas, peeled and halved crosswise and lengthwise
Cinnamon, to taste
¼ cup banana liqueur
⅓ cup light rum
½ cup chopped pecans
Ice cream, for serving

Blend the brown sugar and butter in a skillet and heat until the mixture bubbles. Add the bananas and sauté until tender. Sprinkle with cinnamon. Combine the banana liqueur and rum. Heat slightly, ignite, and pour over the bananas. Baste with the flaming liquid until the flame burns out. Sprinkle with pecans. Serve each person 2 banana halves over scoops of ice cream.

In the South, "fried" or "flamed" bananas were first prepared in the cook houses behind plantation homes. New Orleans restaurants regularly featured this dessert.

=*Robert Mondavi Napa Valley Moscato Bianco*

ABIGAIL VAN BUREN

Enjoy, Enjoy!
Abigail Van Buren
A.K.A.
"Dear Abby"

PHILLIPS VAN BUREN ©

The saga of Dear Abby began in 1956 when Abigail Van Buren, a newcomer to the San Francisco area, called the editor of the *San Francisco Chronicle* and told him she could write a better advice column. To her surprise he challenged her to write replies to some of their previously published columns. She did, and the rest is history. Dear Abby's success was instant. She became nationally syndicated in less than two months because of her wit, wisdom, and commonsense approach. Today she is a household name. She is the most widely syndicated columnist in the world. In addition to writing 365 columns a year she has authored six best-sellers and she still finds time to devote her energies to a number of causes such as the National Foundation of AIDS Research (founding director), equal rights for women and the mentally ill, and as an advocate for the humane treatment of animals. Abby's clout is incredible! One of her most significant accomplishments has been to publicize the concept of the living will. Largely due to her efforts, an estimated fifteen million Americans now have living wills.

Abby's Famous Pecan Pie

NONE BETTER!

(Serves 8 to 10)

1 cup light corn syrup
1 cup (packed) dark brown sugar
3 eggs, slightly beaten
⅓ cup butter, melted
⅓ teaspoon salt
1 teaspoon vanilla extract
One 9-inch unbaked pie crust
1 heaping cup pecan halves
Whipped cream or ice cream, for topping (optional)

Combine the corn syrup, brown sugar, eggs, butter, salt, and vanilla in a large bowl; and mix well. Pour the filling into the pie crust and sprinkle with pecan halves. Bake at 350 degrees for 45 to 50 minutes, or until the center is set and a toothpick inserted in the center comes out clean. Let cool. If the crust or pie appears to be getting brown, cover with foil for remaining baking time. Top with a bit of whipped cream or ice cream or leave plain. Nothing tops this!

= *Robert Mondavi Napa Valley Moscato Bianco*

ISAAC MIZRAHI

Isaac Mizrahi graduated from Parsons School of Design after which he apprenticed with Perry Ellis, Jeffery Banks, and then Calvin Klein before opening his own business in 1987. He has been called the "Wonder Boy" and the "Seventh Avenue Darling." What began as a few pieces a decade ago has rapidly grown into an internationally renowned collection of women's wear, men's wear, a shoe line, and accessories line. He made his film debut in 1993 in *For Love or Money;* in 1995 he was in the highly acclaimed documentary *Unzipped.* He has been recognized for his work in AIDS support.

DEWEY NICKS

Chocolate Mousse

(Serves 4)

4 ounces unsweetened chocolate
¾ cup sugar
¼ cup water
5 eggs, separated
1 teaspoon vanilla extract

Combine the chocolate, sugar, and water in the top of a double boiler. Heat until the chocolate has melted completely, stirring occasionally. Add the egg yolks, one at a time, while the double boiler is still on the heat, beating hard after each addition. Remove the mixture from heat and let cool. Beat the egg whites in a clean bowl until stiff, then blend in the vanilla. Fold the whites into the chocolate mixture, gently but thoroughly. Pour into 4 dessert bowls and refrigerate for 4 to 6 hours.

> Chocolate mousse is the highlight of dinner. It should become what sorbet is now—a mandatory course in between courses.

= *Robert Mondavi Oak District Cabernet Sauvignon*

LEEZA GIBBONS

Leeza Gibbons, successful television host, radio personality, producer, reporter, mother, and wife, has a special and distinctive flair that has won her international recognition. Leeza was honored with a star on Hollywood's Walk of Fame. As host and producer of her own radio and talk shows, she has become a tremendous success. She is actively involved in numerous charities, including the Muscular Dystrophy Association (MDA), American Red Cross, Mothers Against Drunk Driving (MADD), and the March of Dimes. She is an ardent supporter of AIDS causes.

LEEZA GIBBONS ENTERPRISES/PARAMOUNT PICTURES

Mocha Almond Biscotti

(Makes about 5 dozen)

4 cups all-purpose flour
2 cups sugar
2 teaspoons baking powder
1 teaspoon baking soda
½ teaspoon salt
3 eggs
3 egg whites
1 teaspoon vanilla extract
2 tablespoons unsweetened cocoa powder
4 teaspoons instant coffee dissolved in 2 tablespoons hot water
2 ounces unsweetened chocolate, melted and warm
1 cup blanched almonds, toasted
½ teaspoon almond extract

Sift together the flour, sugar, baking powder, baking soda, and salt. Whisk together the eggs, egg whites, and vanilla. Combine with the dry ingredients. Divide the dough into 2 equal portions. Add the cocoa, dissolved coffee, and melted chocolate to one portion. Add the almonds and the almond extract to the other. Divide each portion into 2 parts. Using I part from each portion form a log with the flavors side by side, about 14 × 3 inches. Repeat with the remaining 2 parts. Place on a nonstick baking sheet. The dough is soft and sticky, so use flour on your hands when forming the logs.

Bake at 325 degrees for 20 minutes. Remove and let cool slightly. Slice each log into individual biscotti about ¼ to ½ inch thick. Bake again for 30 minutes, or until dry and crisp. Store in airtight containers. (These will last for several weeks.)

=*Robert Mondavi Coastal Cabernet Sauvignon*

ADAM WYLIE

Adam Wylie is best known for his part as Tom Skerritt's son on the acclaimed TV series "Picket Fences."

CRAIG T. MATHEW

Adam Wylie

Strawberry Pop Cake

(Serves 8)

1 box Duncan Hines Moist Deluxe Yellow cake mix
1 large box (6 ounces) strawberry Jell-O
1 cup strawberry pop
1 cup hot water
1 box (5.1 ounces) vanilla instant pudding
1 tub (8 ounces) soft cream cheese
1 large tub (12 ounces) Cool Whip
½ cup milk
Fresh strawberries, sliced

Bake the cake as directed. While the cake is baking, mix the Jell-O, pop, and hot water and set aside. Let the cake cool. Poke holes in the cake with a fork and spoon the Jell-O mixture over it. For frosting, mix the vanilla pudding, cream cheese, Cool Whip, and milk in a bowl. Spread on the cake and put sliced strawberries on top. Refrigerate for a couple of hours. (This can be made 24 hours ahead for an even moister cake.)

 =La Famiglia Moscato Bianco

LINDA EVANS

Linda Evans started her acting career at Hollywood High with a big break in 1965 when she landed the role of Audra Barkley in *The Big Valley*. During her unforgettable reign on "Dynasty" as the lovable Krystle Carrington, she won five People's Choice Awards and a Golden Globe Award. Among her film credits are *Standing Tall*, *The Gambler, Part II— The Adventure Continues*, and *The Gambler Returns: Luck of the Draw*. Linda is committed to helping women achieve healthy lifestyles. In 1992 she opened the first Linda Evans Fitness Center. In addition to fifteen centers she has a workout video and motivational tapes.

Peach Heaven

(Serves 6)

2 pounds peaches
1½ cups heavy cream
1 tablespoon vanilla extract
1½ cups (packed) brown sugar

Put the peaches in boiling water for 2 to 3 minutes. Peel, pit, and slice them. Put the peaches in a glass baking dish large enough that they fill the dish only halfway. Beat the cream with the vanilla in an electric mixer until thick. Spoon the cream over the peaches. Put in the freezer for 2 hours.

Take the peaches out of the freezer and put a thin layer of brown sugar on top of the cream. If 1 ½ cups isn't enough, add more. Put under the broiler, as close as possible to the heat, and melt the brown sugar, constantly watching. When the cream starts popping out the top, it is done.

Tip: Do not leave the peaches in the freezer longer than 2 hours because when you broil the dish, it will not cook correctly if it has been in the freezer too long.

 =Robert Mondavi Winery Moscato d'Oro

DOLLY PARTON

Dolly Parton is a musician, singer, actress, and songwriter. She is genuinely smart and funny, qualities that have made her one of the most famous celebrities in the country. Her films include *9 to 5* with Jane Fonda and Lily Tomlin and *Steel Magnolias* with Julia Roberts, Sally Field, Shirley MacLaine, Daryl Hannah, and Olympia Dukakis.

DOLLYWOOD FOUNDATION

Stack Pie

(Serves 10 to 12; makes two 3-layer cakes or one 6-layer cake)

6 cups self-rising flour
½ teaspoon baking soda
½ pound (2 sticks) butter
4 eggs, beaten
½ cup molasses
1 cup sugar
1 teaspoon vanilla extract
1 teaspoon cinnamon
⅔ cup milk

FILLING
1 pound apples, peeled, cored, and sliced
½ cup sugar
¼ teaspoon cinnamon
⅛ teaspoon allspice

Sift together the flour and baking soda, add the butter, and mix well. Beat together the eggs, molasses, sugar, vanilla, cinnamon, and milk. Add the flour mixture and mix until it looks like bread dough. Turn out onto a floured board or cloth and knead for a few seconds. Divide the dough into 6 equal parts and roll each out into a thin round like a pie crust. Grease and flour 6 round cake or pie pans. Put 1 round into each pan and pat flat. Bake at 300 degrees for 10 to 15 minutes. Remove from the pans and let cool.

Cook the apples slowly in ½ cup water until soft. Strain. Add the sugar, cinnamon, and allspice. Cook over low heat until the sugar is dissolved and the mixture is thick. Spread the filling on each layer and stack 1 layer on top of the other. This cake is best after it sits for 2 to 3 days.

 = Robert Mondavi Winery Moscato d'Oro

J. CYNTHIA BROOKS

Cynthia Brooks is best known for her role in "Days of Our Lives" as the wisecracking cop, Taylor McCall. She has also produced one film and four theater productions, winning several drama critic's awards. Cynthia composed a full-scale ballet by age thirteen and has won numerous awards for acting and writing. She has appeared in more than thirty theater productions. In mid-1997 Cynthia completely cured herself of a high-grade viral cancer using only alternative medicine. She has been commissioned to write a book on the techniques she applied to her recovery; it is due out in 1999. She is currently starring in *Long Nights,* a feature film.

J. CYNTHIA BROOKS

Hungarian Palascinta

2 cups all-purpose flour
1½ cups sugar
1 teaspoon salt
3 eggs, beaten
2 cups milk
1 apple, finely grated
Margarine or butter, melted, for cooking
Cottage cheese or jelly, for filling

Mix the flour, sugar, salt, eggs, and milk together until the batter is smooth. Add the apple. Thinly pour the batter into a heated pan coated with melted margarine or butter. Tip the pan to spread the batter evenly to the edges. When the underside is golden brown, carefully flip the pancake to turn and brown the other side. Remove from the pan. Stack the pancakes on a large dish. Serve hot or cold. Spread cottage cheese, jelly, or both in the middle of a pancake, then roll it up. It may be cut into halves or quarters to serve.

This is an old Hungarian family recipe handed down from Gypsy mother to Gypsy daughter for generations—never written down, in case they had to flee angry villagers without warning. Family tradition has it my great-grandmother passed it on to my grandmother while driving their troika across the steppes pursued by wolves, occasionally tossing a stolen candelabra at the ravening beasts to distract them. It is said the pancakes work better than any love potion at raising amorous spirits—but then, Grandma only had eleven children. Enjoy!

= Robert Mondavi Winery Napa Valley Fumé Blanc

VINCE GILL

Vince Gill's six albums have all sold a million copies or more. His recognition for outstanding work as a writer, singer, and guitarist include eight Grammys, seventeen Country Music Association awards, and five Academy of Country Music awards. Vince grew up in Oklahoma, the son of a banjo-playing federal judge. He is one of the hottest country music touring acts.

VICTORIA PEARSON

Peanut Butter Fudge

(Makes about 3¼ pounds)

4 cups sugar
2 cans (5 ounces each) evaporated milk (1¼ cups)
½ pound (2 sticks) butter
1 package (10 ounces) peanut butter chips
1 jar (7½ ounces) marshmallow cream
1 cup finely chopped peanuts
1 teaspoon vanilla extract

Line an 8 × 8 × 2–inch baking pan with foil, extending foil over the edges. Butter the foil and set aside. Butter the sides of a heavy 3-quart saucepan. Combine the sugar, evaporated milk, and butter in the pan. Cook and stir over medium-high heat to boiling. Clip a candy thermometer to the side of the pan. Cook and stir over medium heat to 236 degrees (softball stage), about 12 minutes. Remove the saucepan from the heat and remove the thermometer. Add the peanut butter chips, marshmallow cream, peanuts, and vanilla and stir until the peanut butter chips are melted. Spread in the baking pan. Score into squares while warm. When firm, cut into squares. Store in the refrigerator.

= Robert Mondavi Winery Moscato d'Oro

TOM JONES

TIMOTHY WHITE/TOM JONES ENTERPRISES ©

Tom Jones is one of the most enduring personalities in the music entertainment business. He has sustained his popularity for more than three decades. Some of his hit singles are "What's New Pussycat?" "Help Yourself," "I'll Never Fall in Love Again," "Delilah," and "She's a Lady." He has sold more than 30 million discs in all categories. Tom enjoys a regular U.S. and international touring schedule throughout the year. If you ever have a chance to see him perform, don't miss it—he will leave you breathless!

Brandy Snaps

(Makes about 3 dozen cookies)

¼ pound (1 stick) sweet butter
1 cup (packed) light brown sugar
⅓ cup dark corn syrup
1 cup plus 3 tablespoons sifted all-purpose flour
½ teaspoon ground ginger
1 tablespoon brandy

FILLING
1 cup heavy cream
2 tablespoons sugar
2 teaspoons brandy

Melt the butter, brown sugar, and corn syrup in a saucepan over medium-low heat, stirring with a wooden spoon. When the mixture begins to boil, remove from the heat. Stir in the flour and ginger until smooth. Add the brandy. Drop by the half-teaspoonfuls 3 inches apart on a greased baking sheet. Bake at 350 degrees, watching closely, until golden brown, but not dark. While these are baking, prepare a second baking sheet. When you remove the first batch from the oven, pop the second batch in. Repeat until all the batter is used. Let cookies cool for 30 to 60 seconds. Working quickly with a spatula, shape the cookies into a horn-of-plenty shape.

For the filling, whip the cream until stiff. Add the sugar and brandy. Beat for a few seconds. Do not fill the shells more than 30 minutes before serving. You can also serve the shells and cream separately.

=*Robert Mondavi Napa Valley Pinot Noir*

JAMIE FARR

Jamie Farr is best known as Klinger in the hilarious comedy series "M*A*S*H." He started acting and writing variety shows in high school. Jamie was discovered by an MGM talent scout at the Pasadena Playhouse. That won him his first film role— Santini in *The Blackboard Jungle*. A two-year stint in the army took him to Japan and Korea, making him the only member of the "M*A*S*H" cast to have actually served there. Jamie has appeared on TV, in nightclubs, dinner theaters, and films. His films include *Cannonball Run* and its sequel. In April 1985, he received a star on the Hollywood Walk of Fame. In addition to being an accomplished actor and director, he works with a number of charities.

JAMIE FARR

Jamie Farr

Whiskey Cake

(Serves 10)

1 box yellow cake mix, without pudding
1 box (3½ ounces) instant vanilla pudding
4 eggs
1 cup milk
1 shot of whiskey (1½ oz.)
½ cup oil
1 cup walnuts

TOPPING
¼ pound (1 stick) butter
1 cup sugar
½ cup whiskey

Combine the cake mix, pudding, eggs, milk, whiskey, oil, and walnuts. Mix for 3 minutes, then pour into a greased and floured tube pan. Bake at 350 degrees for 50 to 60 minutes. Remove cake from the oven, but leave the cake in the pan.

To make the topping, melt the butter, add the sugar and whiskey, and cook until the sugar is dissolved and the mixture is syrupy. Poke holes with a meat fork in the top of the cake. Pour about two thirds of the syrup over the cake and let stand for 20 minutes. Remove the cake from the pan and pour the remaining syrup over the cake.

 = Robert Mondavi Winery Moscato d'Oro

BUZZ ALDRIN

Buzz Aldrin

Apollo 11 astronaut Buzz Aldrin is the man who uttered the first words spoken by a human being on the surface of the moon. He is now very active in many space exploration activities and has written an excellent science-fiction novel, *Encounter with Tiber*. He is especially good with young people because of his ability to simplify complex subjects. Buzz is a dedicated skier and scuba diver. He hopes to expand his culinary talent with a new recipe, Mars Pie.

Peanut Butter Moon Pie

(Serves 10 to 12)

1 small package (3 ounces) cream cheese
1 cup confectioners' sugar
½ cup crunchy peanut butter
½ cup milk
1 tub (8 ounces) Cool Whip
Two 9-inch prepared chocolate pie crusts
¼ cup finely chopped peanuts
½ cup finely chopped semisweet chocolate bits

Whip the cream cheese until soft and fluffy. Beat in the sugar and peanut butter. Slowly add the milk and blend thoroughly. Fold the Cool Whip into the peanut butter mixture. Pour into the pie crusts. Sprinkle with peanuts and chocolate bits. Freeze or chill thoroughly. Can be served frozen.

 *= Robert Mondavi Winery Moscato d'Oro*

BEVERLY GARLAND

This has been a favorite for years in our family. It came from my mother-in-law, and she would not share it with anyone until she reached her eighties. So this was really hard to come by. We love it.

☆

Beverly Garland was a leading lady of Hollywood films in the Fifties. She subsequently appeared in many TV shows and co-starred with Fred MacMurray in the popular series "My Three Sons." In the late Sixties she returned to the big screen in character roles. Her films include *D.O.A.*, *Where the Red Fern Grows*, *The Mad Room*, and *Pretty Poison*.

HARRY LANGDON

Chocolate Ladyfingers Ice Box Cake

~~~

4 ounces unsweetened chocolate
1 cup granulated sugar
6 eggs, separated
½ pound (2 sticks) sweet butter
1½ cups confectioners' sugar
2 tablespoons vanilla extract
2½ dozen ladyfingers
Sweetened whipped cream, for topping
Chocolate decorations, for topping

Melt the chocolate in the top of a double boiler. Add ¼ cup water and the granulated sugar. When thick, add well-beaten egg yolks. Let cool.

Cream the butter with the confectioners' sugar and add the chocolate mixture and vanilla. Fold in stiffly beaten egg whites.

Line the bottom and sides of a greased 9- or 10-inch springform pan with ladyfingers and pour the mixture into the pan.

Arrange the remaining ladyfingers attractively on top. Refrigerate overnight. Serve topped with sweetened whipped cream and chocolate decorations.

 = Robert Mondavi Coastal Cabernet Sauvignon

TIPPI HEDREN

Tippi Hedren, a former New York fashion model with more than twenty films and numerous television appearances to her credit, starred early in her career in Alfred Hitchcock's *The Birds*. She also co-starred with Marlon Brando in *A Countess from Hong Kong*. Tippi is involved with a number of charitable causes including Food for the Hungry and the USO. She developed an interest in wild animals in 1969 while filming *Satan's Harvest* in Africa. This has resulted in a deep involvement with conservation to save wildlife and prevent cruelty to domestic and wild animals. In establishing the Roar Foundation's Shambala Preserve in California, she has provided a home for abandoned and abused animals including elephants and big cats as well as smaller creatures. This high-desert game preserve is a nonprofit center for big-cat care and research. As founder and president of the preserve, Tippi finds her greatest challenge today is obtaining funds to continue the foundation's work.

Tippi Hedren

Marnie's Favorite Red Velvet Cake

(Makes 1 layer cake)

½ cup shortening
1½ cups sugar
2 eggs
2 cups all-purpose flour
3 tablespoons unsweetened cocoa powder
½ teaspoon salt
1 cup buttermilk
2 ounces red food coloring
1 teaspoon baking soda
1 tablespoon vinegar
Frosting (recipe follows)

Cream the shortening and sugar together until light and fluffy. Beat in the eggs. Sift together the flour, cocoa, and salt. Combine the buttermilk and food coloring. Add the dry ingredients alternately with the buttermilk mixture to the creamed mixture. Dissolve the baking soda in the vinegar and fold in. Turn batter into 3 greased and floured 8-inch layer pans. Bake at 350 degrees for 25 minutes, or until done. Use a cake tester to tell. Cool on racks. Fill and frost.

Frosting

(Makes about 3 cups)

1 cup whole milk
4½ tablespoons flour
¾ cup butter
4½ tablespoons shortening
1¼ cups sugar
⅛ teaspoon salt
3 teaspoons vanilla extract

radually add the milk to the flour in a saucepan and mix until smooth. Bring to a boil, stirring until the mixture thickens. Let cool. Cream the butter, shortening, sugar, and salt together until fluffy. Beat in the vanilla. Combine the cooked milk mixture and the creamed mixture. Chill. Use to fill and frost the layers.

 = Robert Mondavi Napa Valley Cabernet Sauvignon

Acknowledgments

Thanks to the following people, whose help and unwavering support have seen this project to completion:

My parents, Doris and Alvin Dorn, for helping with the logistics and financing and for the thankless task of translating my dyslexic writing into real English.

My sister and brother-in-law, Linda and Chauncey Uphoff, for their help in editing and organizing the manuscript.

My agents, Muriel Nellis and Jane Roberts, who believed in me and steadfastly encouraged me during preparation and assisted me through the quagmire of the publication process.

My brother, Eric Dorn, technical advisor and Webmaster for www.starchef.net.

Robert Mondavi Winery for their support of the project.

My acquiring editor, Sue Carswell; Mitchell Ivers, my current editor; Amanda Ayers; Felice Javit; Laurie Cotumaccio; Amy Rogers; Martha Reddington; and all my friends at Pocket Books.

Finally, all the celebrity contributors who have so generously given of their time and favorite recipes to ensure the success of this book and its major goal—to support a successful search for a cure for AIDS.

Matrix of Wine and Food

Wine	Foods	Sauces, herbs, and seasonings
Fumé Blanc	gravlax, clams, mussels, oysters, sole, salmon, prawns, chicken	cilantro, chives, parsley, shallots, dill, tomato vinaigrette, lemon, herb sauces
Chardonnay	salmon, crab, prawns, scallops, lobster, chicken, quail	basil, saffron, flavored olive oils, seasoned or herb butters, creamy or buttery white sauces with light lemon accents
Pinot Noir	lamb, chicken, duck, pork, game birds, salmon	basil, garlic, cooked tomato sauces, mushroom meat sauces, Aioli sauce, spicy herb sauces
Cabernet Sauvignon	beef, lamb, venison	rosemary, bayleaf, sage, garlic
Merlot	duck, lamb, beef, pork	thyme, balsamic vinegar, orange zest
Zinfandel	beef, venison, duck	garlic, cooked tomato sauces, rich meat sauces
Moscato d'Oro	seasonally fresh fruit: strawberries, raspberries, pears, peaches	lemon and orange zest, raspberry sauce

Fruits and vegetables	Menu recommendations
bell peppers, fresh tomato	poached seafood, lightly grilled seafood with slightly piquante sauces, assorted vegetable-based appetizers, goat cheese (chèvre)
corn, mushrooms, chanterelles, olives	grilled chicken or veal with herb butter; scallops with chardonnay, basil sauce; pasta dishes; prawns with tomato, olive oil and garlic; risotto
root vegetables, mushrooms, tomatoes	roast chicken, grilled firm- fleshed fish (e.g., tuna, salmon, swordfish), rack of lamb, ratatouille
peppers, eggplant, green beans, black currants	roast beef, rack of lamb, aged cheeses
cherries, peppers	roast turkey, roast pork, beef and lamb stews
peppers, eggplant, tomatoes	grilled or barbecued meats, pasta with grilled vegetable or tomato sauce, pizza, cheeses
berries, summer fruits	fruit tarts, frest fruit plates, sorbets

Index

Albert, Eddie, 32–33
Aldrin, Buzz, 254–55
Allen, Steve, 94–95
Alman, Isadora, 68–69
almond
    biscotti, mocha, 239
    brie appetizer, -berry, 19
amaretto caramel custard (flan con
    amaretto), 225
appetizers
    brie, almond-berry, 19
    cheese roll, nutty, Marty's, 15
    chicken fingers, crispy oven-
      baked, 7
    chicken wings marinara, Uncle
      Louie's, 9
    crab cakes, Guillaume, 13
    crab cakes, pan-fried, 3
    lasagna rolls, 5
    salmon, 11
apple(s)
    cake, Rolonda's shakin' quakin'
      cakin', 223
    muffins, -bran, 199
    stack pie, 245
applesauce, 185
artery bread, 211
artichokes, chicken charisma, Phyllis
    Diller's, 59
arugula salad with black olive and
    white bean crostini, 49
avocado, Mérida salad, 41

banana(s)
    bread, blu'bana, 197
    Southern plantation, 234

barbecue(d)
    chicken, 91
    meatballs, B-B-Q, 139
    sauce, 91
    sauce, B-B-Q, 139
    shrimp for two, 141
bass, Chilean sea, 87
bean(s)
    black, and rice salad, 39
    chili, hot and spicy, 143
    soup, and vegetable, Brinkley's
      beautifying, 35
    white, and black olive crostini,
      with argula salad, 49
beef
    Bolognese sauce, 147
    bourguignon, 137
    chicken-fried steak, 111
    chili, hot and spicy, 143
    city chicken, Shirley's, 133
    meatballs, B-B-Q, 139
    pepper steak à la Jane Russell, 107
    picadillo, 81
    pot roast dinner, 169–70
    rice, stuffed, 97
    shepherd's pie with, 83
Berry, Halle, 18–19
biscotti, mocha almond, 239
biscuits, perfect, 207
black bean and rice salad, 39
black-eyed peas, and turkey with
    couscous, supremely healthy,
    181–82
Blackwood, Nina, 174–76
blueberry bread, blu'bana, 197
Bolognese sauce, 147

brandy snaps, 251
bran muffins, apple-, 199
bread(s)
    artery, 211
    biscuits, perfect, 207
    blu'bana, 197
    corn, Southern, 195
    cranberry nut, 203
    monkey, 205
    muffins, apple-bran, 199
    power loaf, famous, 201
bread crumbs, kale with garlic and,
    sautéed, 191
Brinkley, Christie, 34–35
broccoli
    lasagna, vegetable, 85
    pasta à la passion, Joy's, 103
    pasta with leeks and, Joanna's,
      159
    with rigatoni, 73
    soup, cream of, with no cream,
      29
Brooks, J. Cynthia, 246–47
Brown, James (JB), 130–31
Burger, Mike, 74–75
Bush, Barbara, 90–91

cabbage, steamed, 185
cake(s)
    apple, Rolonda's shakin' quakin'
      cakin', 223
    cheesecake, orange chocolate, 219
    chocolate ladyfingers ice box, 257
    custard, 231
    red velvet, Marnie's favorite,
      259–60

cake(s) *(cont.)*
 stack pie, 245
 strawberry pop, 241
 whiskey, 253
caramel amaretto custard (flan con
  amaretto), 225
Carter, Rosalynn, 28–29
Caryl and Marilyn, 210–11
casserole
 chicken curry, 55
 eggplant, 93
Charmaine Lewis's fish escabeche
  with fruity salsa, 79
Chase, Chevy, 84–85
cheese
 brie appetizer, almond-berry, 19
 eggplant casserole, 93
 lasagna rolls, 5
 pierogie, 166–67
 roll, nutty, Marty's, 15
cheesecake, orange chocolate, 219
chicken
 à la Gaynor, 155
 barbecued, 91
 charisma, Phyllis Diller's, 59
 curry casserole, 55
 fettuccine with, 77
 fingers, crispy oven-baked, 7
 garlic thyme grilled, 125
 hash, favorite, 57
 kumquat, 163
 lucky, Mike's, 75
 one-pot poultry passion, 167
 pasta à la passion, Joy's, 103
 salad, Mérida, 41
 silver and gold, 65–67
 soup, curried, 27
 soup, favorite, 37
 spectacular, 129
 spicy, 53
 stir-fry, vegetable, 113
 sweet and sour, Isadora's, 69

 tandoori, Reza's, 157
 wings, marinara, Uncle Louie's, 9
 zingin' singin' Melba Moore's, 145
chicken-fried steak, 111
Chilean sea bass, 87
chili, hot and spicy, 143
chocolate
 cake, ladyfingers ice box, 257
 cheesecake, orange, 219
 chip cookies, 215
 mousse, 237
city chicken, Shirley's, 133
Clark, Dick, 22–23
cobbler, fruit, fresh, 227
Cole, Kenneth, 16–17
Collins, Jackie, 219–20
Collins, Joan, 20–21
compote, fruit, venison, braised,
  with, 117
cookies
 biscotti, mocha almond, 239
 brandy snaps, 251
 chocolate chip, 215
 lace, 217
 oatmeal, Sally's, 229
corn bread, Southern, 195
corn soup, 33
couscous, turkey and black-eyed
  peas with, supremely healthy,
  181–82
crab
 bake imperial, 131
 cakes, Guillaume, 13
 cakes, pan-fried, 3
cranberry nut bread, 203
Cromwell, James, 190–91
crostini, black olive and white bean,
  with arugula salad, 49
cucumber
 gazpacho soup, 31
 salad, Lee's, 45
curry(ied)

chicken casserole, 55
chicken soup, 27
chicken, spicy, 53
custard
 amaretto caramel (flan con
  amaretto), 225
 cake, 231

Damone, Vic, 118–19
DeLuise, Dom, 72–73
desserts
 bananas, Southern plantation,
  234
 custard, amaretto caramel (flan
  con amaretto), 225
 fruit cobbler, fresh, 227
 fudge, peanut butter, 249
 mousse, chocolate, 237
 palascinta, Hungarian, 247
 peach heaven, 243
 rice pudding, Aunt Emma's
  New England, 221
 see also cake(s); cookies; pie(s)
Diffie, Joe, 128–29
Diller, Phyllis, 58–59

Eastwood, Clint, 177–79
Eber, José, 136–37
Eden, Barbara, 54–55
eggplant
 casserole, 93
 Japanese, Lazy Six, 189
eggs and toast for the well-shod
  male, 17
escabeche, fish, with fruity salsa,
  Charmaine Lewis's, 79
essence of silver and gold, 67
Evans, Linda, 242–43

Fairchild, Morgan, 114–15
Farr, Jamie, 252–53
Feinstein, Michael, 98–99

Ferrare, Cristina, 48–49
fettuccine
    with chicken, 77
    in pepper cream sauce, 121
fish
    Chilean sea bass, 87
    escabeche with fruity salsa,
        Charmaine Lewis's, 79
    red snapper, Pacific, 115
    salmon appetizers, 11
    salmon in pastry with herb
        sauce, 175–76
    sole Cabernet, 105
    sweet-and-sour, baked, 172–73
    tuna pasta, spicy, 135
    see also shellfish
Fisher, Frances, 30–31
flan con amaretto (amaretto caramel
        custard), 225
Ford, Betty, 196–97
Frann, Mary, 116–17
Freeman, Kim Fields, 150–51
french fries, great, 151
fruit
    cobbler, fresh, 227
    compote, venison, braised, with,
        117
    rum pot, 187
    salsa, fish escabeche with,
        Charmaine Lewis's, 79
    see also specific fruit
fudge, peanut butter, 249

Gabor, Zsa Zsa, 126–27
Galan, Nely, 230–31
Garland, Beverly, 256–57
garlic
    chicken, thyme, grilled, 125
    kale with bread crumbs and,
        sautéed, 191
Gaylord, Mitch, 134–35
Gaynor, Gloria, 154–55

gazpacho
    pasta, 153
    soup, 31
Getty, Estelle, 6–7
Gibbons, Leeza, 238–39
Gifford, Kathie Lee and Frank,
        198–99
Gill, Vince, 248–49
Glaser, Garrett, 220–21
Gless, Sharon, 156–57
goulash, Dracula (székely gulyás),
        127
Grant, Lee, 184–85
Gray, Linda, 38–39
Guillaume, Robert, 12–13
gumbo, shrimp, 89
gummy bears, spaghetti with,
        123

Hackett, Buddy, 171–73
Hale, Barbara, 10–11
Hamilton, George, 214–15
Hartley, Mariette, 70–71
hash, chicken, favorite, 57
Hedren, Tippi, 258–60
Hefner, Hugh, 168–70
Henderson, Florence, 4–5
herb sauce, salmon in pastry with,
        175–76
Holm, Celeste, 26–27
Holzapfel, Lee, 44–45
Hope, Bob, 56–57
Hungarian palascinta, 247
Hurley, Elizabeth, 62–63

ice box cake, chocolate ladyfingers,
        257
Ingels, Marty, 14–15

Johnson, Lady Bird, 216–17
Jones, Dean, 194–95
Jones, James Earl, 86–87

Jones, Shirley, 132–33
Jones, Star, 208–09
Jones, Tom, 250–51
Judd, Ashley, 206–07

kabobs, city chicken, Shirley's, 133
kale with garlic and bread crumbs,
        sautéed, 191
Karan, Donna, 124–25
Kasem, Casey, 24–25
Kentz, Marilyn, 210–11
Kerns, Joanna, 158–59
Kirkland, Sally, 148–49
Kristensen, Caryl, 210–11
kumquat
    chicken, 163
    sauce, sweet-and-sour, 163–64

LaBelle, Patti, 140–41
lace cookies, 217
ladyfingers chocolate ice box cake,
        257
lamb
    shanks, 101
    shepherd's pie, 63
Lansbury, Angela, 200–01
lasagna
    rolls, 5
    vegetable, 85
Lawrence, Tracy, 138–39
Leach, Robin, 64–67
Le Clerc, Jean, 42–43
Lee, Michele, 108–9
leek(s)
    pasta with broccoli and,
        Joanna's, 159
    soup, and pheasant, 21
Leeves, Jane, 82–83
Leigh, Janet, 100–01
Leno, Jay, 8–9
linguine and clams, 119
Loveless, Patty, 202–03

McGovern, Maureen, 226–27
MacLaine, Shirley, 36–37
marinara chicken wings, Uncle
    Louie's, 9
Meadows, Audrey, 188–89
Meadows, Jayne, 94–95
meatballs, B-B-Q, 139
Meredith, Burgess, 46–47
Mérida salad, 41
Meriwether, Lee, 192–93
Miller, Nolan, 232–33
Mizrahi, Isaac, 236–37
mocha almond biscotti, 239
monkey bread, 205
moon pie, peanut butter, 255
Moore, Melba, 144–45
Moreno, Rita, 80–81
mousse, chocolate, 237
muffins, apple-bran, 199
mushroom
    salad, fresh, 43
    soup, 23
mustard sauce, tiger shrimp in,
    Sally's, 149

nacho salad, Meredith Malibu, 47
Nichols, Nichelle, 60–61
nut(s)
    almond, biscotti, mocha, 239
    almond-berry brie appetizer,
      19
    cheese roll, Marty's, 15
    cranberry bread, 203
    pecan pie, Abby's famous, 235

oatmeal cookies, Sally's, 229
olive(s)
    black, and white bean crostini,
      with arugula salad, 49
    Mérida salad, 41
    spaghetti Boyriven, 71
orange chocolate cheesecake, 219

palascinta, Hungarian, 247
pancakes, Hungarian palascinta,
    247
Parton, Dolly, 244–45
pasta
    à la passion, Joy's, 103
    Bolognese sauce, 147
    with broccoli and leeks,
      Joanna's, 159
    fettuccine with chicken, 77
    fettuccine in pepper cream
      sauce, 121
    gazpacho, 153
    lasagna rolls, 5
    lasagna, vegetable, 85
    linguine and clams, 119
    peppery, 99
    rigatoni with broccoli, 73
    shrimp, à la Zefferelli, 109
    spaghetti Boyriven, 71
    spaghetti with gummy bears,
      123
    spaghetti Western, 178–79
    tuna, spicy, 135
pastry
    salmon in, with herb sauce,
      175–76
    shortcrust, 176
Payton, Jo Marie, 160–61
peach heaven, 243
peanut butter
    fudge, 249
    moon pie, 255
pecan pie, Abby's famous, 235
pepper cream sauce, fettuccine in,
    121
peppers
    beef picadillo, 81
    chili, hot and spicy, 143
    pasta, peppery, 99
    steak à la Jane Russell, 121
Perez, Charles, 96–97

pheasant and leek soup, 21
Philbin, Regis, 102–03
picadillo, beef, 81
pierogie, 166–67
pie(s)
    peanut butter moon, 255
    pecan, Abby's famous, 235
    sweet potato, 209
pork
    Bolognese sauce, 147
    city chicken, Shirley's, 133
    goulash, Dracula (székely
      gulyás), 127
potato(es)
    exploding, 123
    french fries, great, 151
    shepherd's pie, 63
    shepherd's pie with beef, 83
pot roast dinner, 169–70
Potts, Annie, 2–3
Pounder, CCH, 78–79
Powers, Stefanie, 165–67
pudding, rice, Aunt Emma's New
    England, 221

Raphaël, Sally Jessy, 228–29
Reagan, Nancy, 204–05
Reckell, Peter, 112–13
red snapper, Pacific, 115
red velvet cake, Marnie's favorite,
    259–60
Reynolds, Debbie, 92–93
rice
    and black bean salad, 39
    nacho salad, Meredith Malibu,
      47
    one-pot poultry passion,
      161
    pudding, Aunt Emma's New
      England, 221
    stuffed, 97
rigatoni with broccoli, 73

Rivera, Geraldo, 224–25
Roddenberry, Majel Barrett, 162–64
Rudner, Rita, 122–23
rum pot, 187
Russell, Jane, 106–07

salad(s)
    arugula, with black olive and white bean crostini, 49
    black bean and rice, 39
    cucumber, Lee's, 45
    Mérida, 41
    nacho, Meredith Malibu, 47
salmon
    appetizers, 11
    in pastry with herb sauce, 175–76
salsa, fruity, with fish escabeche, Charmaine Lewis's, 79
sauce(s)
    barbecue, 91
    B-B-Q, 139
    Bolognese, 147
    herb, salmon in pastry with, 175–76
    marinara chicken wings, Uncle Louie's, 9
    mustard, tiger shrimp in, Sally's, 149
    pepper cream, fettuccine in, 121
    silver and gold chicken, 65–67
    sweet-and-sour kumquat, 163–64
sauerkraut
    pierogie, 167
    goulash, Dracula (székely gulyás), 127
scallop stir-fry, 61
seafood. see fish; shellfish
shellfish
    clams and linguine, 119

crab bake imperial, 131
crab cakes, Guillaume, 13
crab cakes, pan-fried, 3
scallop stir-fry, 61
shrimp, barbecued, for two, 141
shrimp flambé Newburg, 95
shrimp gumbo, 89
shrimp pasta à la Zefferelli, 109
shrimp, tiger, in mustard sauce, Sally's, 149
spaghetti Western, 178–79
shepherd's pie, 63
    with beef, 83
shrimp
    barbecued, for two, 141
    flambé Newburg, 95
    gumbo, 89
    pasta à la Zefferelli, 109
    tiger, in mustard sauce, Sally's, 149
silver and gold chicken, 65–67
Smith, Liz, 110–11
sole Cabernet, 105
soup(s)
    broccoli, cream of, with no cream, 29
    chicken, curried, 27
    chicken, favorite, 37
    corn, 33
    gazpacho, 31
    mushroom, 23
    pheasant and leek, 21
    vegetable, 25
    vegetable and bean, Brinkley's beautifying, 35
Southern corn bread, 33
Southern plantation bananas, 234
spaghetti
    Boyriven, 71
    with gummy bears, 123
    Western, 178–79

stack pie, 245
steak
    chicken-fried, 111
    pepper, à la Jane Russell, 107
Stevens, Connie, 146–47
Stewart, Alana, 120–21
stir-fry
    chicken vegetable, 113
    scallop, 61
stock, essence of silver and gold, 67
strawberry pop cake, 241
stuffed rice, 97
sweet-and-sour
    chicken, Isadora's, 69
    fish, baked, 172–73
    kumquat sauce, 163–64
sweet potato
    mellow crisp, Kyle and Lesley's, 193
    pie, 209
székely gulyás (Dracula goulash), 127

tandoori chicken, Reza's, 157
Tanner, Lynn, 186–87
Taylor, Elizabeth, 52–53
thyme chicken, garlic, grilled, 125
Tillman, Corliss, 88–89
tomato(es)
    beef picadillo, 81
    Bolognese sauce, 147
    gazpacho soup, 31
    gumbo, shrimp, 89
    Mérida salad, 41
    shrimp pasta à la Zefferelli, 109
tortillas
    nacho salad, Meredith Malibu, 47
    salmon appetizers, 11
Tritt, Travis, 142–43
tuna pasta, spicy, 135

turkey
  and black-eyed peas with cous-
      cous, supremely healthy,
      181–82
  one-pot poultry passion, 161

Van Buren, Abigail, 234–35
veal
  Bolognese sauce, 147
  city chicken, Shirley's, 133
  essence of silver and gold, 67
  goulash, Dracula (székely
      gulyás), 127
vegetable(s)
  chicken, silver and gold, 65–67

gazpacho pasta, 153
lasagna, 85
soup, 25
soup, and bean, Brinkley's beau-
    tifying, 35
stir-fry, chicken, 113
stir-fry, scallop, 61
see also specific vegetables
venison, braised, with fruit com-
    pote, 117
vinaigrette, 49

Watts, Rolonda, 222–23
whiskey cake, 253
Williams, Kellie, 40–41

Wilson, Carnie, 76–77
Wilson, Mary, 180–82
Woodward, Joanne, 104–05
Wylie, Adam, 240–41

yogurt
  broccoli soup, cream of, with no
      cream, 29
  cucumber salad, Lee's, 45
  tandoori chicken, Reza's, 157

Zeman, Jacklyn, 152–53
zucchini, lasagna, vegetable, 85